Poe Dad No Dad

Published by 1123 Publishing Company

ISBN: 979-8-9993429-0-4

Disclaimer: This book is intended for educational and motivational purposes only. It does not constitute professional financial advice. Readers are encouraged to consult with a certified financial advisor before making financial decisions.

Published by 1123 Publishing Company
Knoxville, Tennessee
First Edition, 2025

Poe Dad No Dad

A Blueprint for Freedom, Wealth & Self-Worth

By Almeer Kilee

POE DAD NO DAD: A Blueprint for Freedom, Wealth & Self-Worth by Almeer Kilee, “We weren’t just born in poverty. We were born with the power to escape it.”, Published by 1123 Publishing Company Knoxville, TN. 2025

Disclaimer:

This book is based on real-life experiences, personal growth, and lessons I learned the hard way. It is meant to educate you, inspire you, and spark new ways of thinking, however, it is not professional financial advice. The ideas and strategies shared here are for informational purposes only. Before you make any financial, legal, or business decisions, you should do your own research and speak with a qualified professional.

Table of Contents

Dedication.. iii

Acknowledgments...v

Introduction: The Real Currency is Control................................vi

Chapter 1: Poe Dad...12

Chapter 2: No Dad...21

Chapter 3: More Than One Way Out..34

Chapter 4: The Trap is Bigger Than You Think.............................44

Chapter 5: Game Don't Last Forever..55

Chapter 6: Money Ain't the Answer, But It Opens Doors.....................68

Chapter 7: Own or Be Owned..81

Chapter 8: Rich Starts in the Mind..97

Chapter 9: Use What You've Got to Build What You Need.....................114

Chapter 10: You Are the Asset...124

Chapter 11: Your Story Ain't Over...140

Chapter 12: Real Freedom..157

Chapter 13: Poe Dad No Dad..173

Glossary of Terms.. 186

Templates and Tools...198

About the Author.. 204

Summary………………………………………….206

Acknowledgments

To my children, **Jameerial and Almeer** — thank you for giving me purpose. You are the light that guides every step I take.

To my mother, **Vickie Nance** — we've been through so much. Watching you overcome your struggles gave me the courage to overcome my own.

To my big sister **Tiffany**, my Soul Twin — I love you. Keep shining.

To **Imani Shu'la** — thank you for facilitating people having access to my story.

To my godmother, **Ms. Teresa Duff** — your love and support over the years have been immeasurable.

To **Ms. Stephanie Mason** — thank you for all your help bringing this book to fruition. I'm thankful.

To my **family and friends** — thank you for showing up when so many others didn't.

To attorneys **Jonathan Harwell, Carter Pack, and Melissa C. DiRado** — thank you for standing with me in the fight to reform juvenile justice in Tennessee.

To my friend **Jeremy Young** and the **Al Jazeera English team** — thank you for helping to shine a light on things.

To **Mrs. Adrienne Johnson Martin** — you inspire me. Thank you for all you do.

To the **THEI staff and alumni** — thank you for believing in us.

And last but not least, to **Lonsdale** — there's no place like home.

Introduction:

Poe Dad No Dad is about understanding money. Not just how to get it, but how to keep it, grow it, and let it work for you. It's about waking up from the survival mindset that keeps too many of us broke, broken, or behind bars.

This book is for the kids who were never taught the difference between an asset and a liability.

For the ones of us who grew up thinking fast money was the only money.

For the ones who didn't get trust funds, but developed trust issues.

It's financial literacy in a language you can feel.

It stresses ownership over flexing.

It promotes freedom over fear.

It prioritizes power over pretending.

Because here's the truth. We were never meant to stay poor.

But the system is designed to keep us that way unless we learn the game.

Poe Dad No Dad breaks it down and makes it digestible. In this book you'll learn:

What credit really is and how to protect it

Why your mind is the most valuable asset you'll ever own

How to flip your pain into passive income

How to use smart contracts, digital assets, and compound interest to create real generational wealth

How to build your brand, your business, and your blueprint starting from nothing

This isn't just a motivational book. It's a financial awakening for the kids who never saw themselves in Rich Dad Poor Dad, but still deserve the same opportunity to win.

So if you’ve ever had more ideas than money.

If you’ve ever had to decide between food and the light bill.

If you’ve ever felt like school ain’t teaching you what life actually requires.

Then you're welcome.

This book was written for you.

Because economic empowerment isn’t a dream. It’s a decision.

And by picking this book up, you’ve already started heading in the right direction.

Let’s build.

Chapter 1: Poe Dad

I was the first one that ever called him Poe. Before that, nobody used that name for him. That name came from me.

It started as a joke in my head. “Poe” wasn’t just short for poor. It was Southern slang. The way we say it down here, it sounds like a warning and a nickname at the same time. He was skinny, real lean, but sharp. Dangerous, like a broken bottle. Sleek like a butcher knife. Poe. That’s what I called him, and it stuck, in our hood at least.

He had a real name, of course, but I won’t say it here in this book. Not to protect him from shame, but to protect him from charges. You see, the truth is, a lot of what I’m about to tell you might still get a man jammed up. So let’s just call him Poe and leave it at that.

Now Poe wasn’t my daddy. Not in blood. But in the absence of a real dad, he became something like that. A sit-in. A placeholder. A mirror. A model I looked up to before I realized the difference between real and fictitious.

See, we had what felt like a father and son bond. That's how I viewed it. He looked out for me. Made sure I ate. Talked to me like a man when nobody else even talked to me at all. But underneath all that, he wasn't raising me out of love. He was using me out of convenience. Like a lot of street dudes do with younger kids. He saw in me what the streets love — a body they assume is too young to be charged as an adult, but still capable of following instructions.

When I stole that pack of Now & Laters from Jack's store at ten years old, it wasn't because I was trying to be bad. I was just hungry. Real-life hungry. I got caught though, and that's when he first stepped in.

"Damn, lil' man, you stealin' candy now?" That was some embarrassing stuff, especially because I wasn't even really a thief.

He didn't clown me though. He threw a five-dollar bill on the counter and said, "Keep the change. He's with me."

It felt like a rescue. Like a man swooping in to protect a boy. But looking back, that was recruitment.

He bought me something to eat that day. A cheeseburger, some fries, and a Sprite. I ate like I hadn't had a good meal in days, because I actually hadn't. And he just watched. He didn't talk much at first. But then he dropped something on me I haven't forgotten to this day.

"You know what money is, Meer?" he asked. "It ain't just paper. It's options. It's power. It's leverage. It determines who eats and who gets eaten."

I didn't understand it all then, but it stuck in me like a nail under my skin.

Poe was a hustler. That's what he did. He moved weight. Sold dope to mamas, daddies, uncles, aunties, hell, even mine. He dressed nicely. Clean, he stayed sharp, and always smelled like something expensive. But beneath the fly exterior, he was tired.

Worn down a little. I could see it in his eyes when he thought nobody was looking.

Still, I wanted to be just like him. Because he was the only man I saw who looked like he had any sort of control. But what I didn't know was that he was handing me a weight he didn't want to carry anymore.

He never said, "Meer, go sell this." Not directly at least. But he would ask me to carry things. Drop things. Hold onto bags I didn't want to ask about. And when people came asking, I'd be the one answering. Man, I was carrying pistols before the age of eleven. Just a kid. Protected by age. But disposable to the game.

It took me years to realize that what I thought was mentorship was really manipulation. I wasn't being loved. I was being groomed. I was being used to deflect heat. I wasn't a student. I was insurance.

But here's the twist. I don't hate Poe for that.

Because even in his own flawed way, he taught me something real. He taught me what it looks like to survive without ever having lived fully himself. He showed me the mask that so many men wear. The chains that shine around their necks but really only help to keep them bound. The illusion of control when you're still being chased by the same ghosts every night.

That being said, let's talk about probabilities. Statistically, a Black boy from the inner city has a better chance of going to prison or being killed than becoming a CEO or owning a profitable business. That's not pessimism. That's data. The U.S. Bureau of Justice Statistics says that one in three Black men born today can expect to be incarcerated at some point in their lifetime if current trends continue. One in three. Meanwhile, the number of successful entrepreneurs who come from the hood and make it without selling their soul? You can count them on your fingers in most zip codes.

Now take a figure like Poe. A Poe can influence either outcome. He can increase your odds of survival or speed up your destruction.

He might give you the first meal you've had in days or hand you your first felony before your voice even deepens up. The streets call this a mentorship. But the odds call it grooming.

This is where I teach you something about risk assessment. It's a term from the financial world that applies perfectly here. Investors use it to weigh the potential reward of an investment against its possible loss. What's the upside of carrying weight for a guy like Poe? Some money. Maybe some protection. A sense of belonging. Okay. Now what's the downside? Prison. Death. Losing your youth to a system that profits off your downfall.

A smart investor wouldn't take that deal. So why should you?

That's why understanding probabilities matters. That's also why I'm telling you this story.

One time I saw Poe almost crying. Not in a breakdown way, but just this quiet moment. He was sitting on the back porch of one of his girl's spots, staring off into nothing, smoking a blunt down to the ashes. He didn't see me watching him though. He wiped his eyes. Quick. Like he was swatting at a fly. That's when I realized — even kings bleed. Even gangsters get tired.

Poe never taught me about LLCs. Or credit scores. Or assets. Or compound interest. But he taught me what happens when you don't learn those things. He showed me the burnout that comes with the street game. The paranoia. The hunger that never gets fully satisfied. Because the money is only a form of fast food, but it's actually your soul that's starving.

One night, after a long ride through the hood, he looked over at me and said, "Don't ever wait on another man to feed you, Meer. Learn how to feed yourself, and be sure you own the plate, the spoon, the kitchen, and the recipes too. Don't even drink from another man's cups."

That was the beginning of my awakening.

I started to look at money differently at that point. Not as something to flash, but something I needed to understand. Something I needed to study. Something I could use like a hammer, or a wrench. A tool. Something to flip, multiply, and protect.

Because Poe had a little money. But he didn't have any freedom.

And that's the difference between a street boss and a real boss. One can post bail. The other never has to.

Still, for a kid like me? Poe was everything I had.

Keys to the Chapter: Poe Dad

1. Real Game:

Not every role model is a real model. Some people teach you to survive, but not sustainability. Just because someone feeds you for today doesn't mean they're feeding your future.

2. Financial Focus – Risk Assessment:

A good investor doesn't gamble with high losses and low rewards. You shouldn't either. If the cost of your choices includes prison, death, or losing your youth, it's better to just walk away. The ROI ain't worth it.

3. Action Step:

List three financial moves you're making (or thinking about), and next to each, write the worst-case and best-case outcomes. Then ask: Would a smart investor say yes? Or No?

4. Quote to Carry:

"I wasn't a student. I was insurance."

Let that sit. Then flip it.

"I'm not a pawn. I'm a key player. I make the moves now."

Chapter 2: No Dad

My biological father's name was Humphrey. At least that's what the people in the streets knew him by.

That name carried weight once upon a time. Not just because of who he was, but because of what he could've been. He was one of those rare types. A gifted athlete. A smooth talker. A fighter. A gambler. And a hustler. They say he had hands like a pro boxer and the kind of football talent that could've taken him to the league. That's how good he was. But like too many stories in places like Knoxville, especially in the communities we come up in, talent alone wasn't enough to outrun the streets.

So like so many others, Humphrey got caught up. Caught up in the drugs. The women. The fast life. All of it.

He and my mama must've met when they were around high school age. She was such a dreamer. Short, chocolate, and beautiful. She had a smile that could make a man forget all his troubles. She had goals. He had game. Needless to say, she fell for him. But by the time she got pregnant with my older sister, he had at least two other girls pregnant too. All of them beautiful. All of them fooled.

That kind of betrayal doesn't just hurt a woman. It shifts something inside her soul. Needless to say, my mother was crushed.

He disappeared after that. From what I've heard, he put miles on a lot of cars, working his way across the country. He stayed gone until one day, when my sister was about five or six years old. Out of the blue, she saw him in the neighborhood. She yelled out to him, "Daddy!" He turned around. Came over. And just like that, the fantasy of a family was rekindled in my mother's mind. At least for that night, it was.

From what I've always been told, my sister walked in on them at some point that night. When she did, Humphrey half-jokingly asked her, "Do you want a little brother or a little sister?" She supposedly said, "A little brother," and I guess the rest, as they say, is history.

My mother got pregnant with me that night.

I was conceived in a flash of confusion. From one last spark of something that wasn't ever really love to begin with. It was just a ghost of twisted emotions. The desire for something that was never meant to be. My mama always said I was made in love. But even she knew it was the kind of love that came wrapped in pain.

And Humphrey? He didn't stick around.

I mean, it wasn't like he was abusive. He wasn't loud or boisterous. He was just absent. But don't let that fool you. Absence in itself can be as loud as any argument. It echoes. It carves itself into you almost like the silence has teeth.

See, there's the kind of pain that comes from being hit. And then there's the kind that comes from not being seen at all. It was the latter of the two that I had to endure.

He never taught me how to ride a bike. Never showed me how to throw a punch. How to shake a man's hand. How to open a bank account. I never heard the words, "I'm proud of you." It was my sister who taught me how to tie my shoes. What I got from him wasn't love. It was complete deprivation.

And when boys have a void like that, they try to fill it with all kinds of stuff. Things like gangs. Money. They try to fill it with approval, with bad decisions. I carried that void like a thousand-pound weight in my chest. I walked around wondering, "Was I not enough? Did he ever even care? Am I doomed to be just like him?"

I saw his face every time I looked in the mirror. I saw him walk with every step I took. His shadow was my future. It felt like I was living in a haunted house, and the ghost was me.

But even in his absence, Humphrey taught me things. He taught me how to stand on my own. He taught me that nobody was coming to rescue me. He taught me to be my own man, even if I had to teach myself how to do it.

And somewhere along the line, I made a promise to myself: if I ever had children, it would be different.

I’d be there for them. I’d teach them what he didn’t teach me. No excuses. No matter what.

I'd teach them how to invest. How to manage money. How to protect their peace and harness their power. I'd teach them how to pray. How to build something that lasts.

Because a father doesn’t just provide food to his children. He provides a blueprint. A map to show them the way forward

Now let’s talk numbers. You know I gotta bring receipts.

According to the U.S. Census Bureau:

Children without a father in the house are four times more likely to live in poverty. That’s 400 percent more than children with their dad at home.

They’re twice as likely to drop out of school.

And they’re seven times more likely to end up pregnant as a teenager or incarcerated before adulthood.

Think about that for a second and let it sink in.

The presence of a father, especially one who understands finances, isn't just emotional support. It's economic infrastructure. It's like walking into life with a financial head start. It better equips you for the future.

Children in two-parent households are far more likely to:

Graduate high school and attend college

Maintain higher credit scores

Start investing earlier

Inherit land or wealth

Understand banking, budgeting, and long-term planning

That's not random. That's intentional. Fathers are necessary to a child.

A father who knows about savings accounts teaches his kid to open one early. A father who understands life insurance passes on protection and peace of mind to his next generation. A father with good credit passes down opportunities that can change his children's lives.

Let me give you a real-life example.

A kid I knew from a nearby community had a father who worked construction and made about fifty thousand a year — not rich by any stretch. But his dad taught him how to save. Told him to open a Roth IRA at eighteen and start putting just a hundred dollars a month into it. With compound interest, by the time that kid turns fifty, that small monthly habit could grow to over two hundred thousand dollars.

(A Roth IRA is a retirement savings account that allows you to invest post-tax income, grow your money tax-free, and withdraw it tax-free in retirement.)

Now compare that to a kid who never learned about compound interest. Who never even learned how to budget. Who didn't have a dad to teach him the difference between assets and liabilities, between wants and needs. What does that kid do when he gets his first job? He blows the check.

Not because he's dumb. But because nobody ever taught him any better.

That was me.

I didn't get those lessons at the dinner table. I had to learn them in the field. In jail cells. In courtrooms. In broken relationships and overdraft fees.

You know how expensive ignorance is? It costs dreams. It costs decades of your life.

But that's why I'm here now, giving you the blueprint I never had. Hopefully you're soaking this up.

Let me drop some more high-level game on you, Youngster.

1. Your first investment is your mindset. If you believe you're destined to be like your absent father, you're already losing. Start by believing you can break the cycle. Because you absolutely can.

2. Start early, even if it's small. If you put away fifty dollars a month starting at nineteen in a basic index fund with eight percent annual return, you'd have over $135,000 by age fifty. That's real. The sooner you start, the better.

3. Understand credit. A 720-plus credit score can save you tens of thousands of dollars over a lifetime in lower interest rates on cars, homes, even insurance. Learn to use it. Don't abuse it.

4. Legacy is a strategy. Whether or not you have a dad, become the kind of father (or mother) your children will one day thank for setting them up the right way.

And here's the part we rarely talk about.

The Black family during Reconstruction, right after slavery, was one of the most powerful institutions in America. Despite being recently freed, Black couples were getting married at record rates. Fathers were leading households. Families were building businesses, schools, and communities.

That scared the system.

So here came policies like the welfare restrictions of the 1960s and the mass incarcerations of the 1980s that punished Black families for staying together. In order to receive housing benefits, the man had to be gone. It wasn't just economic — it was cultural warfare. They broke up the home because they knew a strong Black family is the root of generational wealth. These are facts, not opinions.

When the man is removed, the foundation is shaken.

And we've been trying to steady it ever since.

So if you've got a father in your life, one who shows up, who teaches you things, one who provides game — don't take that lightly. That's a form of wealth in itself.

And if you don't?

Then you be the first.

Be the first in your family to open an investment account.

Be the first to build credit the right way.

Be the first to teach your children about money, about ownership, about true peace.

Because the only thing stronger than a curse is a choice.

And to break generational curses, you may have to do things that haven't been done in your family for generations.

But you're built for it.

If not, you wouldn't be here with me now.

Keys to the Chapter: No Dad

1. Real Game:

Absence leaves a scar you can't always see. A missing father isn't just an emotional loss. It's a structural disadvantage. But pain can either be your excuse or your blueprint.

2. Financial Focus — Generational Infrastructure:

A father who understands money doesn't just give you gifts. He gives you a head start. Financial knowledge passed down early is the difference between surviving and building a lasting legacy.

3. Action Step:

If you didn't grow up with a blueprint, start creating one now. Write down three things you wish someone taught you about money. Then go learn them. Use books, YouTube, mentors — whatever it takes. That's how you build your legacy forward.

4. Quote to Carry:

"The presence of a father is emotional support. But it's also economic infrastructure."

Chapter 3: More Than One Way Out

Growing up where I'm from, Lonsdale, a small community in Knoxville, TN, it was easy to believe that the world ended at the edge of the block.

Everything I saw felt permanent, like struggle was built into the foundations of the actual buildings. Abandoned houses, boarded-up windows, pit bulls, sirens, and stray shots in the distance. That low hum of survival vibrating in everybody's chest. You learn fast that everybody has a role they're playing — from the hustlers, to the boosters, to the lookouts, even the users (we used to call them "chronics"). People move with purpose around here, even when that purpose is just to survive.

I was caught right in the middle. Smart enough to stay out of the deep water, but surrounded by a school of young sharks who kept calling me in. And truthfully, part of me wanted to swim with them. I was hungry for respect. For control. For proof that I mattered.

School wasn't a lifeline either, not to me anyway. It felt like a joke. The textbooks were all old and worn out. The teachers were exhausted and unmotivated. Most of them looked at us like we were already statistics. I'd sit in class, head down, hoodie up, half-listening. The only thing that kept me coming back was the free lunch and the chance to stay warm in the wintertime.

They always talked to us about going to college someday. But how can you picture a campus when you've never seen one? How do you dream about a future you've never witnessed? Who ever taught us about FAFSA forms?

(Applications that students fill out to see if they qualify for financial aid to help pay for college.)

SAT scores?

(Standardized test results used by colleges to measure a student's readiness for higher education.)

That felt like a foreign language to me.

But the streets? The streets made promises you could touch today.

Quick money.

Fast respect.

No waiting.

I saw it all up close and personal too. Poe had introduced me to that world without fully pulling me into it. But I could feel it. The temptation of it. The seduction of it. I had friends who were already in deep — making money, wearing chains, flexing on the 'Gram and social media. Meanwhile, I'm at home eating mayonnaise sandwiches and wearing shoes that lean sideways when you're walking straight forward.

It felt unfair. Like the only ones winning were the ones who stopped caring. The ones who found a way to cut corners.

But not everybody was lost.

There was Coach D. A big ashy dude with rough hands and old beat-up sneakers. His voice was rough and scratchy like sandpaper, but his heart — his heart was like gold. He saw something in me. He used to let us run laps with the older kids when they practiced, just so he could talk to us about life afterwards while we were too tired to argue. He'd say things like, "Meer, you got a leader in you. Don't let the hood talk you into being average."

He was the first adult to call me a leader.

Then there was Mrs. Jones, the librarian. Glasses always crooked. She smelled like peppermint. A beautiful woman — inside and out.

One day she caught me pretending to read just to stay in the library and stay warm. She didn't shame me. She simply walked over and slid a book across the table.

The book she slid me was The Autobiography of Malcolm X. She said, "Read it. You remind me of him."

That book cracked something open in my young mind.

I saw myself in Malcolm. A rough start. Often misunderstood. But powerful once focused. He wasn't just surviving. He was transforming — inside and out. Both himself and those around him. That became the seed for something new in my mind.

I started thinking differently.

Started noticing the patterns. The traps.

The way money came fast but left even faster. The way people who flexed hard often fell off the hardest. The way people celebrated your downfall out loud but pretended not to notice your growth. Especially if it didn't directly benefit them in some way.

That's when I learned the real truth.

That there's more than one way out — but only if you're brave enough to look beyond what's right in front of your face. You gotta really step back and see the bigger picture.

I started paying attention to the small opportunities. The ones nobody flexes about. A summer job at a screen-printing shop making T-shirts. Helping a neighbor fix up an old bike. Cutting a yard. Tutoring a younger kid in math.

Each little move, regardless of how small, taught me something: money is about motion. Momentum. Flow. And that motion creates options. Those options present you with different opportunities.

The real flex wasn't the fast car or some jewelry. It was having choices.

You want to know the most dangerous thing in the hood — or anywhere else for that matter?

A man with no options. A man who feels like he has no other choice. There's no scarier sight than the face of a desperate man.

That's who the system fears.

That's who the world tries to contain. That's who they lock away in prisons all across this country.

But give that same man a vision, some game, and a few tools — level the playing field for him, and allow him the same access you allow those who are more like you?

Now you've got a builder. A business owner. A king. Someone to look up to.

Coach D once told me, "You can use money like a weapon or like a shield. It depends on what you're trying to protect or fight."

That stayed with me.

I had always heard, or misheard, that money was the root of all evil. I say misheard because money isn't evil. What's evil is not knowing how to manage it. Not recognizing its potential if used correctly.

You can use it to buy food, or to buy time.

To fund your growth, or waste time trying to flex for people who don't even care.

That's when I decided that I didn't want fast money. I wanted free money. Automatic money. Money I didn't have to struggle for. Money that worked for me while I slept.

And the first step toward that kind of money was to understand that there was more than one way out.

It's easy to tear things up. There are plenty of shooters. There is no shortage of corner boys. It's not hard to play the role everyone else pushes on you.

But how many people will choose the harder route?

The builder's path.

How many people are wanting to do more than just survive?

How many are trying to build something that lasts?

Keys to the Chapter: More Than One Way Out

1. Real Game:

The streets will only show you what's close. But real vision means stepping back far enough for you to see the bigger picture. There's always more than one way out , but only if you believe it exists.

2. Financial Focus , Momentum and Motion:

Money moves. Even the smallest hustle, if managed correctly, can create options. It's not always about how much you make. It's mostly about learning how to let your money work for you and create new doors.

3. Action Step:

Write down three things you could do right now to earn money legally. Don't just think big. Think possible. Then choose one and try it for seven days. Track what you learn, not just what you earn.

4. Quote to Carry:

"The real flex isn't the fast car or the chain. It's having choices."

And the one that hit the hardest:

“There’s no scarier sight than a man with no options.”

Chapter 4: The Trap is Bigger Than You Think

It started with the corner, or the dark cuts between the red brick project buildings. I used to think the trap was just a location, an old abandoned house where the product was moved. A spot on the block where money came quickly but danger came even quicker. I thought it was something you could see — one way streets, crack pipes, hypodermic needles, boarded-up windows, yellow tape, and busted-out street lights.

But I couldn't have been more wrong. The real trap isn't just in the streets. It's in your mind. It's in the broken educational systems. It's in what they tell you you're worth, and what they never bother to teach you at all.

The trap is layered, and leveled.

It's the school building with broken heaters and rotten ceiling tiles. It's the teacher who labels you a "trouble maker" because you speak with passion. It's the principal who suspends you for being frustrated in a world that never gave you peace, or a place of value to belong.

See, they build the trap early. And reinforce it throughout the course of your life.

They build it when they remove financial literacy from the curriculum.

They build it when they celebrate slavery and civil rights as the only chapters Black kids need to learn.

They build it when they show you Columbus before they show you Mansa Musa. (Google him.)

Or when they teach you about the Founding Fathers, but not about the Moors. (Look them up.)

You sit in those desks and start to believe those lies: that your people never built anything, never ruled anything, never invented anything, never led. When in fact they did — for thousands of years they did.

So what do you do?

You shrink.

You act out.

You check out. Clock out.

You fall behind.

And when you fall behind, they push you further away. They label you. Suspend you. Send you home to a single mom who's already juggling responsibilities, habits, and a mountain of bills.

Before I dive into how the system sets kids like us up to fail, I wanna give credit where it's due. A lot of what opened my eyes about money came from Rich Dad Poor Dad by Robert Kiyosaki. In that book, he broke down how schools train you to become an employee, not an owner. They teach you how to clock in, follow rules, and obey orders — but never how to build wealth or think critically about money.

Kiyosaki's "poor dad" had a good education, but stayed broke. His "rich dad" never finished college, but he understood assets, cash flow, and freedom. That contrast helped me realize the trap wasn't just in the hood. It was in the lessons we weren't being taught in school. And for Black and brown kids, that gap is even wider.

Now, if they're teaching the kids on that side of the tracks to be employees and feeding them faulty financial information, imagine what they're doing with the Poe folks. I'll tell you what it is…

It's called the school-to-prison pipeline. They don't always say it out loud, but it's real. You mess up in 6th grade, and they're already prepping your bed in juvie. Or even the penitentiary.

And the streets? They're waiting too.

All these traps make room for the ones who get sent home too many times. They welcome the ones who got tired of being told they weren't enough. The trap becomes attractive to those types, because at least it offers something. Money. Power. Attention. A name.

I saw it firsthand. Boys I grew up with that were brilliant. I mean, they could've been anything. They could've been engineers, coders, designers, leaders. Instead, they were running plays, watching people's backs, holding weight for bosses. You'd be surprised how many times I saw a person with more potential than they gave themselves credit for drop out of school altogether after earning a thousand or two in the streets.

And the cold part? They were still using their brains. The hustle takes intelligence. It absolutely requires you to think. And think fast.

But that intelligence never got nurtured in school. It got mislabeled, medicated, and sometimes even punished.

That's what the trap feeds on though: unfocused genius. And it doesn't stop at school.

Look around the neighborhoods that look like ours: most of them have more liquor stores than libraries. More pawn shops than banks. More fast food than fresh food.

Everything designed to keep us numb, broke, reactive. Everything to keep us trapped.

Even money, something that we should be using to empower ourselves, gets weaponized and used against us.

They teach us how to spend it. Not how to grow it.

They teach us about flexing, but not about flipping.

They tell us to chase the bag, but never how to own the business that makes the bags.

The trap is bigger than just drugs and violence. It's consumerism without any real purpose. It's loyalty to brands that don't know your name or care about your condition. It's measuring your value by what's on your feet instead of what's in your head and heart.

And don't get it twisted, the trap is smart. It's built to adapt. It takes on a new shape, a new form, a new persona, so to speak, with every move you make to get away from it.

If you escape the block, it shows up in your bank account.

If you dodge a bullet, it shows up in your taxes.

If you make it to college, it shows up in your tuition.

It doesn't stop just because you get out the hood.

Because if your mindset never changed, it doesn't matter where your zip code is.

But there is a way out. If you're ready to learn what that is, just keep reading.

It starts with recognizing that you were never the problem. You were born into a system designed to confuse you, to distract you, and to drain you of the best you have to offer.

And once you're able to understand that?

You'll stop being prey. You'll start being more strategic.

I started reading the things they didn't assign in class. Books about wealth, about mindset, about history. I started asking questions they never answered in school. I started watching interviews, learning from other people's pain, absorbing game from anywhere I could get it.

And the more I learned, the more the walls of the trap started to fall.

Because real freedom ain't just about being outside.

It's about being unlocked — in your mind, in your money, in your mission.

The trap wants you to be reactive.

It wants you distracted.

It wants you to think short-term.

But the real win is a long game.

A marathon.

Assets. Ownership. Vision. Generational moves.

That’s why I'm writing this. Because if no one teaches you how to see the trap, you’ll keep walking into it thinking it’s home.

So yeah, look around. See it for what it is.

The trap is bigger than you think.

But so is your future.

And the moment you realize that?

The game will open up to you. Things will change… forever.

Keys to the Chapter: The Trap is Bigger Than You Think

1. Real Game:

The real trap isn’t just the corner or the cut. It’s a mindset, a system, and a design that starts early. If they can confuse you, distract you, and strip you of your knowledge, then they never have to chain you, you’ll stay stuck without them lifting a finger.

2. Financial Focus — Consumers vs Creators:

They train you how to spend, not to build. To flex, not to invest. But ownership flips the script. You don't have to be the buyer forever. You can be the brand, the creator, the asset.

3. Action Step:

List three things you've spent money on in the last month that didn't grow in value. Then list three ways you could turn your own skills or ideas into something people would pay for. Shift your focus from consuming to creating. There's a difference.

4. Quote to Carry:

"The trap is bigger than just drugs and violence. It's consumerism without any real purpose."

And the one that hits the mind:

"Because real freedom ain't just about being outside. It's about being unlocked — in your mind, in your money, in your mission."

Chapter 5: Game Don't Last Forever

To the outside world, Poe looked like a winner.

To me, sitting in the back seat of his Cadillac, windows slightly cracked, with the leather soft and warm under my legs, he was what the game was all about. Gold chain twinkling in the sunlight. The crispiest lineup you ever saw in your life. Waves spinning. Wallet fat. Everybody knew him. Everybody wanted to be him. Or at least, that's how it seemed to me when I was young.

He taught me to keep my posture right, my voice firm, and my chin up. "Confidence makes 'em pay attention," he'd say. "Silence makes 'em wonder." Poe was the kind of man who moved through rooms like he owned the air in there. And in my young mind, I thought that was power.

But there's something they don't show you in the highlight reels.

Poe was running from something.

Not from the law, though that was always hovering close by. Not from some other guys in the streets, he wasn't a sucka, or any type of a coward, but from time, regret, and reality. The money looked good, but it left too fast. The women smiled, but their eyes stayed scanning the exits. Or looking for the next man with money. The cars were clean, but they made it easier to record your movements. And every conversation sounded scripted. Like there was always something left unsaid, questions left unanswered.

The cracks started small.

One of the rides went missing. Then the chains started seeming like they didn't shine quite as bright. Like my guy had stopped twinkling his jewelry. Then Nika came into the picture. She was fly, no doubt, but hungry. And not in a good way. That kind of hunger that steals from your plate while smiling in your face. Poe didn't catch it at first. Or maybe he did, and he was just tired of being alone.

She started stealing from him, first a little weed here and there, then cash, and then jewelry. By the time he finally realized it, it had gotten so far out of hand that there was no way not to notice it. That's when things got physical. He lost it, beat her up pretty bad. It echoed through the hood like a gunshot. Everybody heard about it. And just like that, Poe was gone.

He knocked a new girl and hit the highway with her. A pretty, young, Carmel colored girl with natural hair and big pretty legs. I can't say for sure where he would've found her but she was seriously fine, and dangerously underage.

They disappeared. They hit Houston. Atlanta. The Carolinas. Quick stops. Long nights and early mornings. And for a moment, it looked like he was starting fresh. Like he was finally able to turn things back around.

But the game doesn't just let you start over like that. Not when you never played it clean to begin with.

When he came back he came back different.

All the big pretty cars were gone. All he had left was the Lac'. And it had plenty of miles on it by then. He looked older, even though only months had passed. The edge in his voice had dulled. The hunger in his hustle was gone.

We parked and just sat in silence. No music. Just the tick of the engine cooling down.

"Don't end up like me, Meer," he said finally. "The game don't love you. It only hires you to destroy you."

That line hit me harder than anything he ever taught me.

Because for all the times I wanted to be like Poe, I never realized I was only seeing the highlights. I never saw the receipts. The stress. The betrayal. The pressures of trying to stay alive in a game that feeds off your hopes and dreams.

That was the day I started asking different questions.

Like: If Poe had started a business instead of flipping packs, would he have lasted longer?

If he had bought property instead of chains, would he still have had to run?

If he had learned credit, taxes, and investments, would he be in a Benz, instead of that same old Lac'?

See, there's a difference between money and wealth.

Poe had money.

But he didn't have wealth.

Let me break it down to you like this:

Money is loud.

Wealth is quiet.

Money buys clothes. Wealth buys time.

Money pays bills. Wealth pays for a future.

Nobody taught Poe how to invest. Nobody handed him books on compound interest, mutual funds, business credit, or LLCs. So he played the game he was handed — you know, the cards he was dealt. And like most, he played it well... until he didn't.

That stuck with me.

Because here's what I started learning — and what Poe never got to:

1. Start with Ownership

I learned that your name has value. If you build credit under your name, you can use other people's money (OPM) to fund your dream.

Loans. Credit. Capital.

You don't have to trap to flip. You just need a plan, a name, and a paper trail.

2. Start a Business, Not a Hustle

An LLC costs about $300 in most states. Once you've got it, you can open a business bank account, write off expenses, and build business credit.

Start small. Sell shirts. Cut hair. Do nails. Clean sneakers. Teach younger kids a skill.

Don't chase fast money. Chase scalable money.

3. Learn the 3 Levels of Income

Earned income — working for every dollar.

Passive income — money from assets (like vending machines, online products, books).

Portfolio income — stocks, crypto, real estate. The kind of stuff that makes money while you sleep.

4. Buy Assets, Not Just Stuff

Poe loved cars. But those cars didn't pay his bills.

An asset is something that pays you back:

A rental property

A dividend stock

A course you create and sell online

A T-shirt brand that keeps selling while you're in the studio

5. Get an Emergency Fund

Poe didn't have one. So when things fell apart, he had to run.

A savings cushion gives you some breathing room in the event of an emergency.

It keeps you from falling into desperation when things get rough. And at some point, they always do.

6. Know When to Pivot

Know when to change lanes. Poe stayed in the game too long.

The hustle has an expiration date.

The streets love you today and testify against you tomorrow.

I wasn't trying to go out like that.

So while Poe was fading into the shadows, I started stepping into the light.

Not loud. Not flashy. Just different.

I started reading.

I started writing.

I listened to podcasts on money and financial stuff.

I watched videos on how to start and operate a brand.

I talked to people who'd been through things and came out clean on the other side.

And little by little, I built something.

Not yet a throne.

Definitely not a trap.

But a foundation.

Because I realized something:

Fast money feels good. But smart money lasts a whole lot longer.

And I wanted my story to end with a strong legacy — not catastrophic loss.

So here's the real game:

The streets will always be there.

But so will the bank.

So will the business license.

So will the investment app.

So will the mentor willing to answer your questions.

It’s up to you which line you wanna stand in.

Poe chose speed and flash.

I chose structure and discipline.

Because the game don’t last forever.

But wisdom? Wisdom is undefeated.

And from where I’m standing now?

Wisdom is the real plug.

It’s the supply that never runs dry.

Just read a little more when you're ready to re-up.

Keys to the Chapter: Game Don’t Last Forever

1. Real Game:

Poe looked like he had it all , cars, jewelry, respect. But behind the highlight reel he was exhausted, regretful, and carrying the weight of staying alive in a game that eats its own. The streets give you a mask, not a legacy.

2. Financial Focus — Wealth Over Flash:

Money pays bills. Wealth pays for freedom. Poe had money, but no true foundation. Ownership, structure, and financial literacy are the tools that turn short-term wins into long-term security. Learn the difference

3. Action Step:

Write down one thing you're doing just to look like you've got it, and one thing you could be doing to actually build it. Shift your energy from flexing to foundation.

4. Quote to Carry:

"The game don't love you. It only hires you to destroy you."

And the wake-up call:

"That was the day I started asking different questions."

Chapter 6: Money Ain't the Answer, But It Opens Doors

In the hood, almost everybody has a nickname. Whether it's something you get at home from your closest family members, a name the kids give you on the playground, or like me, one that just attaches itself to you out of unspoken truth. My nickname was Needy. I didn't particularly like that name. It was even embarrassing to be called that in public. But like a lot of things in the streets, it stuck.

I don't think it came about because I begged, but because I never had the basic necessities. By this time, drugs were getting the best of my mom. My sister had already moved out, and me and my younger brother were sharing what little was left behind. Most of the time, that wasn't much. In Lonsdale, being broke wasn't just a financial condition, it was a state of mind. Poverty was no stranger to neighborhoods like ours. It shaped everything. The way we walked. The way we dreamed. The way we spoke.

That nickname stuck like the smell of fried bologna in a house with no ventilation. In the hood, names aren't just names, they're reflections of how people see you. They speak for you before you even open your mouth. And here's what I learned: being broke doesn't just affect your pockets, it affects your choices, your confidence, your vision. Your entire identity.

So when money finally started coming in, legal or not, I didn't take it for granted. Because I didn't just want it. I needed it. Not to show off either. Not for clout. But for genuine survival. To eat. To provide for me and my little brother. And, maybe most of all, to feel like I mattered.

But what I didn't understand back then was this: poverty teaches you how to spend money, not how to grow with it. We're raised and taught to focus on consumption. We're taught early on to spend, and work. We learn how to chase the next hit of dopamine — from shoes, to status, to snacks. But the real players? They're building empires off discipline, game, and a sound understanding of how money really works. It's crazy how we don't see the difference until it's too late.

The truth is, most of what wealthy people do isn't even hidden. It's right there in front of our faces, just never translated into a language we understand. So let me be that translator. Let's take what they teach in Ivy League finance programs and make it digestible in barbershops, cafeterias, and on project porches. Because money ain't the answer, but it can be the key to freedom, if you know how to use it.

Growing up we never had much. Most nights it was rice for dinner, sometimes stretched with ketchup or butter. Other nights it was mayonnaise sandwiches or a piece of bologna fried so thin you could almost see through it. If we were lucky, Mama scraped up enough for hot dogs or a frozen pizza. I ate so many fish sticks. We drank sugar water from old jars because we couldn't always afford Kool-Aid. But hunger didn't just live in my stomach, it lived in my spirit…

I was starving for options.

So when Poe started bringing me around more, I didn't see it as grooming. I saw it as a relief. I held his bags, moved light work from one porch to another, kept an eye out in case the police were coming. It started small. But small things grow. And soon enough, I was "earning." Five dollars off every twenty I made for him.

At the same time, Coach D helped me land my first real job, screen printing T-shirts. Minimum wage, but clean money. The kind that came with a pay stub and a paper trail. I cashed my first check, bought a used PS4, brought home pizza, and stashed the rest in a shoebox under my bed. For the first time, I felt real pride. But I also felt impatience. Because while that job was legit, the street money was faster.

That's when I started living a double life. One foot in the working world, one foot in the streets. One hand pressing a heat press. The other delivering product wrapped in plastic. One version of me wore an apron. The other wore paranoia. I told myself it was temporary. Just a bridge. But the truth is, fast money has gravity. It pulls you deeper while convincing you you're still in control.

And that's when I had to face the question that changed everything:

What does money really mean to me?

Because I knew what it meant to be broke. I knew what it meant to go without. I knew what it meant to want things I could never ask for. But I had to learn the hard way that just having money isn't enough.

You need to understand it. Gain control of it. Make it work for you.

That's where the game shifted for me.

Let me break this down plainly:

Money isn't the end goal. Freedom is.

Money is a tool. It ain't supposed to own you. You're supposed to own it.

There's a difference between being rich and being free.

Poe had moments of being rich.

But he was never truly free.

He was always watching his back, always making runs, always calculating his next move just to stay afloat. That's not wealth. That's stress.

Meanwhile, the world I was waking up to — through books, through how-to videos, and lessons from people like Coach D — was showing me a new path:

The Wealth Game.

Here's a few of those principles:

1. Income vs. Wealth

Income is what you earn. Wealth is what you keep.

Income buys shoes. Wealth buys land.

Income pays bills. Wealth affords you freedom.

You can make $1,000 a day and still die broke if you spend like you're rich and never save anything.

2. Assets vs. Liabilities

An asset is anything that puts money in your pocket.

A liability is anything that takes money out of it.

That chain is a liability. That vending machine, bringing in $200/month while you sleep — that's an asset.

When I finally understood this, I stopped trying to look rich. I started trying to actually be free.

3. Passive Income is the Goal

Money that you're not physically working for.

Could I sell something online?

Could I write something once that pays me again and again?

Could I create something — digital, art, music, ideas — that people would pay for?

4. Digital Wealth is Real Wealth

I learned about crypto, blockchain, and NFTs from my little cousin. He was playing Roblox and showed me how he built a game map and got paid in Robux.

“I made this hat and my friend bought it,” he told me. “But now it’s an NFT. So every time someone else buys it, I still get a piece.”

That hit me like lightning.

You mean... I can create once and continue to get paid forever?

That’s passive income on steroids.

I did my research.

NFTs aren't just pictures. They're digital proof of ownership — art, music, contracts, clothing designs, in-game items. All of it can be turned into assets.

I followed pages on blockchain technology.

I learned about smart contracts — self-executing agreements that trigger once conditions are met.

No middleman. No arguments. Just trust in code.

Now, I treat credit like a weapon.

I build it. I guard it. I use it only when it builds value.

I opened a secured credit card. Bought gas and groceries. Paid it off early. My credit score started to climb.

Then I started thinking bigger.

Could I launch a T-shirt brand using print-on-demand?

Could I drop an eBook and collect royalties?

Could I take this very story and turn it into an NFT, limited-run, so every resale comes back to me?

The answer was yes.

And that's when it hit me:

I don't want fast money. I want money forever.

Money that pays for my future.

Money that funds my mental, spiritual and emotional healing.

Money that puts my mama in a place with a garden and central air.

Money that makes sure my kids will never be called "Needy."

So I started building. Day by day. Plan by plan. Lesson by lesson.

I still mess up. I still get tempted. I still struggle between pride and patience.

But I'm in the game now.

The real game.

The game of financial freedom.

The game of self-mastery.

The game of building wealth in a world that taught me nothing but basic survival.

Keys to the Chapter: Money Ain't the Answer, But It Opens Doors

1. Real Game:

Being broke doesn't just affect your pockets. It chips away at your confidence, your choices, and your sense of self worth. When money finally shows up, it feels like a relief , but if you don't understand it, you'll lose it as fast as you got it.

2. Financial Focus , Survival Money vs Freedom Money:

Fast money has gravity. But real wealth comes from understanding how to use money as a tool, not just how to get it. When you move from survival to strategy, you can stop chasing checks and start building revenue streams.

3. Action Step:

Make a list of what you spend money on, and ask: does this build me up or just keep me afloat? Then write down one small move you can make this week to move toward passive income or ownership — even if it's just watching a video, starting a free account, or writing an idea down.

4. Quote to Carry:

"Poverty teaches you how to spend money, not how to grow with it."

And the shift that changes everything:

"I don't want fast money. I want money forever."

Chapter 7: Own or Be Owned

I remember sitting on the porch outside my apartment one day, just watching people walk down the street. Everybody seemed to have something they were proud of. Whether it was a fresh pair of tennis shoes, the latest cell phone, or a gold chain that caught the sunlight just right. People would post their new outfits on social media and wait to see if the likes went up. And even though I had learned a lot by then about money, assets, and credit, I still felt that pull. That desire to look like I had something, even if it meant I wasn't building anything at all.

That's a trap, because you can look successful long before you ever own success. And if you're not careful, you'll spend way too much of your life chasing the image, never realizing that you were supposed to be creating the actual substance.

Ownership is everything. Always remember that.

I don't just mean owning a house or a car. I'm talking about owning your ideas. They call that your intellectual property. Your voice. Your time. Your identity. That's what (N.I.L.) is all about. Your story. And eventually, yes, your business, your property, and your wealth.

Because if you don't own it, someone else does. And if someone else owns it, they control the terms. They control you.

That's why this chapter is called what it's called.

Own or Be Owned

The Psychology of Consumerism

Ever since you were a child, you've been trained, often without realizing it, to be a consumer. Every cartoon had a toy line. Every commercial was a pitch. Every holiday came with a shopping list. Even on your birthday, you felt like a failure if you didn't buy yourself something new. It starts early. And by the time we're teens, it's already part of our identity.

But here's the thing. They're not just selling you products. They're selling you validation. They're telling you, "If you don't have this thing, you really don't matter."

So what do most people do?

They chase those things.

The newest Jordans.

The latest designer belt.

The newest iPhone.

We go broke trying to look like we're not broke.

We spend hundreds of dollars on brands that we don't own a single share of. We wear their logos proudly, while the people who created them are building legacies off our money.

That's not hate. That's just the game.

The real question is this.

When are we going to flip the roles?

When are we going to make the transition from Consumers to Creators?

When are we going to become the providers of our own products or services?

Here's something I want you to remember forever:

If you can make people believe in something, you can build a brand.

It doesn't have to be big.

It doesn't have to be perfect.

But it has to be yours.

I created a shirt with my own design. It wasn't perfect, not at all. The fabric was basic. The cut was off. But when I put it on and wore it around, people asked about it. They saw my confidence while wearing it. They saw my originality.

They saw ownership.

When you own something, whether it's a design, a product, or simply just a vision, it shifts how people look at you. But more importantly, it shifts the way you look at yourself.

So ask yourself, what is it that I already know how to do well enough that I could turn it into a brand?

Can you cut hair? Record music? Design clothes? Edit video? Can you cook, write, draw, repair bikes, build apps?

That's a skill. That has a value. That's currency.

And when you turn it into something consistent, you can package it. You can own it.

That's power.

What Does It Mean to Own Something?

Let's make this practical. Here are five things you can start owning right now:

1. Your Story

Nobody else can tell your story better than you can. Journal your experiences. Speak your truth. Use it as the foundation for your brand. People want to know about it.

2. Your Name

Secure your name as a web domain. Even if you're not ready to use it yet. That's digital real estate, just as valuable as physical real estate.

3. Your Ideas

Document everything. Start a notebook or a folder on your phone. The more ideas you collect, the more value you build.

4. Your Online Presence

Lock in your social handles across platforms, even if you don't use them yet. That's equity.

5. Your Time

Time is the one commodity you can never get back once it's spent. So be picky about how and where you spend it. Time is money. That's why jobs pay by the hour.

And if you're ready to level up?

Start looking into trademarks, business licenses, and EINs. Learn how to turn your brand into an entity.

Here's why that matters.

When you turn your passion into a registered business, you unlock a whole new world. Business credit, tax deductions, legal protection, and generational possibilities. A business entity is almost like owning the rights to a whole other person. The entity can own property, have assets, credit, a bank account, all of its own. Totally separate from your personal stuff. Like an extra man on the playing field.

Cultural Ownership: Who Profits Off You?

Let's get even deeper.

I don't think anyone could dispute the fact that Black and brown culture drives trends. From music to fashion to slang, we influence everything.

But who owns it?

It's wild how we create the drip but rarely own any of the faucets.

We set the trends. We originate style. We orchestrate the sounds. And yet, when you look at who owns the record labels, the fashion brands, the platforms, we're not on the deeds.

We're the engines, but not the owners.

That has to change. Don't you agree?

It starts with valuing your ideas. Stop giving your flavor away for free. If you have a catchphrase, trademark it. If you're designing flyers, add a watermark. If you're building an audience, direct them to a product that you control.

Don't let someone else take your blueprint and build a castle with it.

Digital Real Estate Is Actual Real Estate

Back in the day, if you owned land, you had power.

Today, you can own land in the physical world and also in the digital space. The online world has just as much land, if not more, than the physical world.

Here's what digital ownership looks like:

Owning your domain name (YourName.com)

Owning your brand name across all major platforms

Owning your content (YouTube videos, eBooks, music, digital art)

Creating NFTs to monetize your creativity

Don't let the tech terms scare you. This is just like setting up shop on your block. Only this block is global and online.

When you own your corner of the internet, you're not just creating — you're controlling.

And when you control the territory, you control the profits. You protect the bag. You scale up. You expand your reach.

High-Level Financial Game: Licensing and IP

If you're serious about owning your work, you need to understand licensing and intellectual property (IP).

Licensing means someone pays you to use your creation or your ideas. They don't own it. You do. But they pay you to use it.

Intellectual property includes your brand name, logo, original content, slogans, and even your story if it's unique enough.

Imagine this. You design a logo that catches fire. A local artist wants to use it. You license it. They pay to use it. You still own it.

Or you write a short story. Someone wants to turn it into a film. You get paid. But you still keep ownership.

That's how the wealthy stay wealthy. Not by trading time for money, but by creating assets that keep working even when they're not.

Sound familiar?

That's what we talked about in the last chapter — forever money.

Ownership makes that possible.

Spiritual and Emotional Ownership

Now let's bring this home.

You can own your brand. You can own your business. You can own your time.

But none of it matters if you don't own yourself.

Own your decisions.

Own your mistakes.

Own your healing.

Own your growth.

Too many of us are renting personalities we saw online or swagger we saw someone else make look good. We borrow lingo. We mimic vibes. We chase applause from people who don't even know us.

But when you walk in your truth?

Nobody can buy you.

Nobody can clone you.

Nobody can cancel you either.

They can't break you because they didn't make you.

Because you know who you are.

And you know what you're building.

Closing Game: Build What Can't Be Taken

Here's what I want you to take from this chapter:

You don't need permission to create.

You don't need money to start a brand.

You don't need fame to be valuable.

You don't need to chase what was never meant for you.

What you do need is to take yourself seriously, even when the world doesn't.

Because one day, someone's going to look at you and say,

"They really built something out of nothing."

But it won't be nothing.

It'll be your name. Your mission. Your message.

Your brand. Your movement. A foundation for generations to come.

So go ahead.

Start small.

Start now.

Start something of your own.

Because in this life, you either build the table or wait to be offered a seat at somebody else's. And there's not even a guarantee that you'll like what's being served.

And I'd rather teach you how to build your own table.

Even hire your very own personal chef.

One brick. One word. One move at a time.

Own or be owned. The choice is yours.

Keys to the Chapter: Own or Be Owned

1. Real Game, Ownership or Servitude

You either build your own table or you end up eating off someone else's. True power isn't in wearing a logo — it's in owning the logo, the brand, and the story behind it.

2. Financial Focus, Intellectual Property and Digital Assets

Your ideas, your name, your creations — these are real assets worth more than any designer label. Treat your story, your designs, and your online handles as property you protect and monetize.

3. Action Step

Write down three skills or ideas you already have. Next to each, note one way you could turn it into a product, service, or digital asset you own (for example a simple e-book, a branded social handle, or a small product drop). Then choose the easiest one to launch this week.

4. Quote to Carry

"If you don't own it, someone else does."

"Own or be owned."

Chapter 8: Rich Starts in the Mind

I remember one day I was walking past an old boarded-up house on Minnesota Avenue. I wasn't really looking for anything special to happen, I'd walked past this spot a thousand times. It was a bando. The windows were busted out. The siding was peeling. Weeds had started growing up through the porch. It was like the earth was trying to reclaim the whole lot. Most people didn't even look at it. Just another forgotten property on a forgotten section of the block.

But that morning, there was this older dude standing in front of it. He sorta looked like he'd just been released or something. He had on baggy khakis, state-issued boots, and a fresh glint in his eyes. He was standing there like he owned it. Holding a notebook, pacing the sidewalk, nodding to himself.

I slowed up a little and asked him, "What you doing out here, OG?"

He looked up at me and smiled a little bit. He said,

“I’m just visualizing the blueprint, Lil Homie.”

He said he was gonna turn that house into a multi-unit rental property. He said he’d already drawn up the plans, already talking to the contractors, already got his EIN, and was working on getting the deed.

It blew my mind.

Because where I saw just a run-down, old, abandoned house, he saw developable real estate.

Where I saw a trap house, he saw a foundation.

Where I saw history, he saw future equity.

That’s when it hit me:

Your mindset is the lens that defines your reality.

He wasn’t crazy. He was just locked into a vision that most people couldn’t see yet. That’s what mindset does. It shifts your frequency. It tunes you in to things that are invisible to others — like Wi-Fi.

Your thoughts are the architects of your future.

The things you see in your mind today will determine how you move Tomorrow

The Trap Is More Mental Than Physical

Let me break this down for you plain. Your mindset is the headquarters for your hustle. Ground zero. You can't build anything lasting without starting there. You can get a little money. You can get some followers. You can even get some respect. But if your mind ain't right, none of those things will last.

You see, your mind is like a radio.

Whatever frequency you're tuned into will determine what music will play on your channel.

If you're locked on 98.3 "Fear FM," you'll see threats everywhere.

Tuned to 102.7 “Hustle & Hope,” you’ll find doors where other people see walls.

Does that make sense to you?

Rich is a mindset, way before it's numbers in a bank account.

You can be dead broke and still carry yourself like someone destined for greatness. That’s not delusion. That’s direction.

And I ain’t talking about faking it until you make it either. I’m talking about calling things that aren't as though they already are.

That's powerful stuff.

Most of the people I grew up with were smart. Talented. Sharp.

But they were stuck mentally.

Not because they were lazy, but because they never learned to allow themselves to see more than what was physically in front of them. They were mentally fenced in.

Fenced in by what they thought they couldn't be.

Fenced in by what the school system said they would never be.

And fenced in by all the pain they never got help unpacking.

The biggest prisons don't have bars.

There's no place that's harder to escape from than your own mind.

And if you believe that the only way to win is to hustle, flash, and flex, then you'll never sit still long enough to build anything.

The biggest shift in life starts when you realize mindset isn't just important — it's foundational.

Have you ever heard of Wallo267?

This brother did 20 years in prison.

Came home, got on Instagram with nothing but his phone, started dropping gems, speaking truth.

He built his platform from the floor up.

He co-founded the “Million Dollaz Worth of Game” podcast with his cousin, Gillie da Kid.

Now he’s in rooms with CEOs, athletes, and millionaire investors.

That’s not magic. That’s the power of mindset.

He walked out of a cell and saw a wide open world.

He shifted the whole narrative.

He turned his experience in the prison system into a press run.

Turned his pain into a platform.

Look at 50 Cent. Everybody knows his story. He got shot nine times. He could've been dead. He didn’t quit. He could’ve easily spiraled into drugs or depression. Instead, he transformed himself into one of the biggest stars the rap industry has ever witnessed — music, clothing, TV, legacy.

Look at Jay-Z. Another brother that came from nothing. He too built something the industry said couldn't be done — ownership, partnerships, generational wealth.

They all share one thing in common:

They tuned in.

They didn't listen to the noise or the static in between the stations.

They focused, adjusted their mindsets, and locked in.

From Survival to Strategy

Most of us were raised strictly to survive.

Watch your back.

Stack your money.

Don't talk too much.

Stay dangerous.

That's a survival mindset.

And it works — for a while. Until it doesn't.

Survival teaches you how to protect yourself.

But it doesn't teach you how to position yourself.

You can't build real wealth from fear.

You have to build it from faith.

From focused vision.

From supreme confidence.

You've gotta switch gears.

From surviving this one day,

To designing the next decade.

From "I hope I make it,"

To "I'm building something big."

That's the mindset.

Mental Currency: Make Your Thoughts Pay Rent

Here's another way to think about it.

Your mind is like a luxury condo.

Every thought you have is a tenant.

So who are you allowing to live in your building?

And at what cost?

Self-doubt?

Shame?

Jealousy?

Procrastination?

Do you have enough room for:

Strategy?

Gratitude?

Vision?

Execution?

Just like a landlord has to be selective about choosing their tenants, you have to be selective about choosing your thoughts.

Because it's your tenants who determine your property value.

Here's Some Practical Game to Help You Build a Rich Mindset

1. Start the day in peace.

Sit in silence before you scroll. Reflect on the fact that you're alive. All the money in the world is worthless if you're not here to enjoy it. Be thankful.

2. Write daily intentions.

"Today I'll finish that beat."

“Today I’ll read 10 pages.”

Your intentions shape your actions. Your actions become your routines. Your routines shape your future.

3. Speak life into yourself.

Out loud. Every morning.

There is power in your spoken word.

Many faiths believe words created the world.

Words are magic — that’s why they call it “spelling.”

4. Cut distractions.

Mute negativity. Control your mental feed.

You can’t enjoy the music if you’re listening to five stations at once.

5. Feed your mind.

Watch documentaries. Learn. Be intentional.

If you want your mind to grow, water it. Your mind is a muscle. Exercise it often.

6. Practice gratitude.

List 3 things you're thankful for every day.

Gratitude determines your altitude.

The Deepest Wealth Is Knowing Who You Are

There was a night I laid in bed scrolling IG.

Everybody flexing. Dubai. Lambos. Designer.

And for a second, I felt small.

Like I'd never get there.

Like I wasn't doing enough.

But then I caught myself.

What am I chasing?

Peace or performance?

Purpose or popularity?

I'm not in competition with strangers.

I'm in alignment with my assignment.

I realized something powerful:

You stop leasing your self-worth when you remember who you are.

You stop renting your confidence when you own your self-awareness.

It ain't what's on you — it's what's in you.

And that's the kind of wealth nobody can tax.

Closing Game: The Wealthiest People Master Themselves First

You can have the money. The followers. The platform.

But if your mind isn't ready for it,

how will you maintain any of it?

That's why this chapter matters.

Because the mansion starts with a mindset.

The empire starts with an inner vision.

The legacy starts with your thoughts.

So ask yourself:

Are you tuned in to survival or strategy?

Are you consuming or creating?

Are you playing to impress or to make an impact?

Your mind is a vault.

It holds your plans.

It holds the keys to every door.

The sooner you clean out the clutter and build from within,

the sooner the world around you changes.

You don't need permission. You need a new perspective.

You don't need luck. You need to lock in and focus.

You don't need perfection. You need vision.

Because the wealth, the freedom, the peace —

It all starts in one place:

Your mind.

Let that be the first asset you invest in.

Everything else is just the interest on your original investment.

Rich starts in the mind.

Start thinking like that.

Start living like it.

Start building like it.

Right now.

Keys to the Chapter: Rich Starts in the Mind

1. Real Game

Mindset is the first currency. Before you get the money, you have to master your mentality. Broke isn't just a financial condition, it's a spiritual one too. The trap isn't always physical. Sometimes it's how you think, it's what you believe, and what you settle for.

2. Financial Focus

Mental wealth is the foundation. Money without mindset is just chaos with commas. The real rich think in terms of assets, time, peace, and purpose. Start training your thoughts the way you would train for a fight , with discipline, focus, and vision.

3. Action Step

Start your morning with three minutes of silence. Then write down one thing you're building and one thought that's been potentially holding you back. Replace that thought with a new one. Speak it out loud. Lock in.

4. Quote to Carry

"You stop leasing your self-worth when you remember who you are."

Let that echo in your chest. Rich starts in the mind.

Chapter 9: Use What You've Got to Build What You Need

In the hood, most people think you need a million dollar plan to get started. They think you need an investor, a perfect pitch, or a verification badge to win. But I've seen the truth up close. And the truth is this — the ones who build themselves to be the biggest often start out the smallest.

I'm talking about people like Twin, the Candy Lady.

Every hood has one. Ours lived two buildings down from me in Lonsdale. No big signs. No uniforms. No menus. Just a fold-out table, a deep freezer, a couch, and a whole lot of hustle.

She had everything you could want as a kid. Pickles. Quarter bags of chips. Frozen cups of Kool-Aid. Hot sausages. Now & Laters. Microwavable nachos. She didn't have a storefront, just a tiny apartment that smelled like hot grease and corn syrup. She even had single cigarettes and cigars for the people who wanted them.

We'd line up outside her door after school with coins, EBT change, and sweaty dollar bills balled up in our fists. She made her rent like that. Probably helped a grandbaby or two eat off that little setup.

No Shopify.

No startup money.

Just supply, demand, hustle, and dedication.

But it wasn't just grown-ups who had that mindset. I remember my big sister, back when we were little, used to do her own version of the Candy Lady hustle.

She was maybe in middle school, and we didn't have much. But she got smart. She took the Kool-Aid we already had in the house, some sugar, a couple of Styrofoam cups, threw that in the freezer overnight and — bam. Freeze cups. She charged a quarter apiece.

Then she started baking peanut butter cookies in the tiny oven in our kitchen. Just a few batches at a time, wrapping them up in plastic sandwich bags.

She wasn't making hundreds. But she was making something. Enough to buy herself a school shirt. Enough to grab a snack when Mama couldn't. Enough to remind herself she wasn't powerless.

That stuck with me. I respect it to this day.

She didn't wait for permission. She used what was already in the house. And that's the game.

Start where you are.

Use what you have.

Build until it grows.

The Myth of "Needing More"

Everybody's waiting on something.

A better phone. A fancy camera. A newer laptop. An industry cosign. More followers. A big advance check.

But I'm telling you the power is already in your hands.

If you've got a phone, then you've got a business.

If you have an idea, you have a potential product.

If you have a story to tell, then you've got a brand.

We live in a time where you can start with zero dollars and still find a way to eat. And eat well.

That's the blessing. And the test.

Real Life Example: Improving What Already Exists

Let's look at someone who took an existing idea and flipped it.

Have you ever heard of Virgil Abloh? Rest in peace. He was the creative director of Louis Vuitton and founder of Off-White. But before all that, he was just a kid from Illinois who loved fashion.

He didn’t invent fashion. He didn’t invent streetwear.

He didn’t invent graphic design.

What he did was combine them in a new way. He took the simplicity of luxury branding and married it with street culture. He put quotation marks around words on hoodies. He called things what they already were. He’d put the word “SHOELACES” on shoelaces, or “SCULPTURE” on bags.

It was a remix.

But it hit like a total revolution.

Virgil proved something vital:

He proved that you don’t have to create something new. You just have to create something true to your style.

Let’s Talk Financial Game

Now that we’ve covered the creativity, let’s get into the currency.

Here are a few real tools you can use to turn your hustle into an income stream, starting with little to no capital.

1. Leverage

Leverage is using what you already have to get what you need.

You don't have to own everything. Sometimes it's about who you know, what you know, or what you can offer.

Let's say your cousin has a van and you're good at organizing. You partner up and start a moving service. You schedule and promote. He drives. You both carry luggage. You split profits. That's leverage.

Or say you have a social media following, and someone else has a product but no audience.

You promote. They provide. You both eat.

2. Dropshipping

You've probably heard the term, but maybe didn't know what it meant.

Dropshipping is when you sell products online without holding any inventory.

You build a store using free platforms like Etsy or Facebook Marketplace. People order from you. The product ships straight from the supplier to the customer. You never even touch it.

Your profit is the difference between what the customer pays and what the supplier charges.

Sell a phone case for $20. Pay the supplier $8. You just made $12 without touching a box.

3. Arbitrage

Arbitrage means buying low and selling high.

Anything with more value than what you paid for it can qualify. For example:

Buying shoes on clearance and flipping them online

Going to Goodwill and finding rare items to resell

Buying candy in bulk and selling it at school (if they let you)

The key is market awareness — knowing what's hot, where to get it cheap, and where to sell it for more.

Compound Interest Revisited

Let's look at compound interest again with real math.

Start saving $50 a month at age 19. You invest it in something with an 8% annual return (very possible in long-term stock market investing).

By age 40, you'll have over $32,000.

Only $12,600 of that is your actual money.

The rest — over $19,000 — is pure interest.

Now keep going until age 60. That becomes over $150,000.

Start with $100 a month instead? That's over $300,000.

Small seeds grow big trees.

Keys to the Chapter: Use What You've Got to Build What You Need

1. Real Game

The blueprint doesn't always come from a boardroom. Sometimes it starts with a deep freezer and a dream. You don't need a perfect plan, just the courage to start. Hustle isn't about what you don't have, it's about using what's already in your hands.

2. Financial Focus

Small money when done right beats big money done wrong. Freeze cups and peanut butter cookies might seem minor to you, but they teach the same lessons as a multimillion-dollar business. Supply, demand, consistency, and reinvestment. Wealth is built from the ground up.

3. Action Step

Look around and list three things you already have access to — a skill, a resource, or a tool. Write one way each could be used to earn money or provide value. Then pick one and make a move this week. Creativity over capital.

4. Quote to Carry

“She wasn’t making hundreds. But she was making something.”

Let that be the reminder. Motion beats perfection. Start where you are and build from there.

Chapter 10: You Are the Asset

Aye, if there was one key life lesson that I wish someone would've put me up on when I was younger, it would be this:

You are your very first, and most critically important investment. Before anything else. You.

Not the clothes you wear.

Not your online followers.

Not a fancy car or some exclusive kicks.

You.

Your mind.

Your physical health.

Your spiritual well-being.

And most definitely the name and reputation you build for yourself.

Most people spend the majority of their younger years chasing what they think they need to make themselves feel whole—money, respect, love, power. But what if I told you that all those things, everything you're looking for, is right there inside of you already, written into the very fabric of your DNA. It's just waiting to be developed, like equity in a rehabbed property.

So this chapter isn't just going to be motivational. It's also going to be financial. It's going to be strategic. But most of all, it's going to be real.

Because in today's world, the most powerful asset isn't gold or silver. It isn't oil or Bitcoin. It's not real estate. It's not artificial intelligence.

It's self-worth. It's the value that you hold within. Especially when it's backed by knowledge of self and ownership of your God-given place in creation.

The Cost of Not Knowing Your Value

Too many of us are taught to simply try to survive, but never taught how to protect what we carry within.

When you don’t understand your worth—your real value—you're more likely to commit these types of mistakes:

Spending yourself into debt by trying to impress people who don’t really care in the first place.

Staying in circles that take away from your value instead of cultivating or adding to it.

Trading your freedom for attention.

Joining groups and affiliations that look like love, but are actually costing you your future.

Gangs look really attractive to those who have never grown to understand their individual self-worth.

People looking for a place to belong will often overlook the purest form of love available to man—self-love.

And I’ve seen it up close and personally:

I've seen kids get themselves locked up for stealing clothes and accessories—all because they thought these things made them matter more in some way.

I've seen teens and young kids join gangs because they felt like it was the only place they could truly be seen, heard, or respected.

I've seen little girls getting pregnant just trying to show that they were worthy of a little male attention—just trying to feel loved.

Little boys dying over comments on social media. Over chasing clout. I've watched so many of my friends die over street names, corners, and communities they didn’t even own.

That’s not just sad. It’s expensive too.

Because all that time, energy, and potential we lose—as a culture, as a community, and ultimately as a society—it can’t be refunded.

But when you do know your value, you can then begin to make better investments.

Think Like You're a Business

Ok. Let me break it down to you another way:

If your life was a Fortune 500 company, what kind of asset would you be?

You are the brand.

Your name is your reputation.

Your energy is your engine.

Your body is the product.

And your decisions? Your decisions are investments.

So, would you invest in you?

Would any smart investor look at you, at your day-to-day habits and say, “That’s someone I could believe in”?

Would your future self thank you—or would he be trying to recover from the decisions you're making today?

Every choice you make today is either building or taking away from your future value.

Your time is currency—be careful where and how you spend it.

Your health is capital—there's tremendous value in staying fit and in shape.

Your attention? That's your stock portfolio. The things you focus on most are the things most likely to show up more in your life.

Stay focused on the right things.

Don't give anything up too cheap.

High-Value Assets Protect Themselves

Let's talk a little bit about risk management, because successful businesses always plan for unforeseen setbacks.

1. Your Physical Health

Drugs, pills, alcohol, stress—all these things are like high-interest debt on your body.

They cost you more than just the moment. They rob you of your drive, your confidence, your performance.

A smart man wouldn't put cheap gas in a Ferrari. Stop putting poison in a body that's built for greatness.

2. Your Mental Health

Anxiety, trauma, confusion—these things are like viruses in your operating system.

If left unchecked, they could crash your whole system.

Prayer, therapy, meditation, journaling, talking things out—that's maintenance.

Don't wait until your system is broken down to value your mental clarity.

3. Emotional Decisions

Acting out of pride, ego, pain, or peer pressure is how a lot of people lose.

You don't want to throw your whole brand in the trash over one heated argument.

Step back. Think about the long-term. That's how CEOs move.

Today's Society: The Trap Is Flashy, Freedom Is Silent

In today's culture, the loudest people online often have the least equity in real life.

Fake flexing is at an all-time high.

Self-investment is down.

But those who win aren't necessarily the loudest.

They're the most intentional.

While everyone else is chasing likes and public approval that they'll never even attempt to monetize, the ones of us that are serious about this game are building credit.

We're registering LLCs.

We're learning tax codes.

We're staying drug-free because we want to pass background checks.

We're protecting our options.

Because in this economy? Options are everything.

And data backs all this up:

Statistics will show you that young entrepreneurs of color are the fastest-growing group of new business owners.

Personal branding is one of the top ways people are building wealth, most of them without ever stepping foot onto a college campus.

Skills like coding, marketing, content creation, and digital sales are allowing people to turn phones into fortunes—especially post-COVID.

That means the battlefield is shifting.

It's no longer just about street smarts or school smarts.

It's about self-value and adaptability.

Understanding Your Worth, and then Multiplying It

Here's how you invest in yourself like the asset you are:

1. Learn a skill you can sell

Whether it's braiding hair, computer coding, cutting grass, making beats, editing videos, painting, flipping shoes—it doesn't matter. Just develop one skill you can charge for.

2. Build credit like your last name depends on it

Keep your name clean too. Get a secured credit card. Pay it off.

Learn what credit utilization means.

(It's like your reputation score in the money world.)

3. Learn your value in relationships

If someone doesn't respect your time, your goals, your healing, your peace of mind—they're a liability, not a partner.

4. Control your circle

Birds of a feather still flock together.

If your circle ain't growing, your dreams won't either.

Your networks are a form of credit in themselves.

Knowing and being linked to the right people could take you far—just as being tied to the wrong people could bring you crashing down.

5. Invest time, not just effort

Energy without structure is chaos.

Time without direction is waste.

Create routines that reward your future.

Everything you do has the potential to be habit-forming.

Make it a habit to dedicate time to the things that can elevate your status.

Long-Term Thinking: Your Future Self is Watching

When you start valuing yourself, your decisions become different.

You won't just put yourself in any situation. You'll have something to lose.

You start asking:

Will this decision cost me years I can't get back?

Will this post help my image or potentially hurt my brand?

Will this purchase affect my future credit score?

That's legacy-level thinking.

And once you start thinking that way, you become almost unstoppable.

Because everyone else is playing checkers, while you're building a whole chessboard.

Final Word: You Are Not Just a Product of Your Past or Your Environment

You are an investment.

A brand.

A blueprint.

You were not born just to survive.

You were born to have dominion.

To grow.

To stretch.

To scale.

To live abundantly.

And I don't care how broke, how hurt, how overlooked you started out.

You are not too far gone.

You are not too damaged.

You are not too late.

Your story is still in draft form.

And the pen is in your hands.

You are the asset, Youngster.

So protect your value.

Grow your worth.

And move like someone who can't be replaced—because there will never be another you.

If you lose a bag, you can get it back.

But if you lose yourself, you lose everything.

Keys to the Chapter: You Are the Asset

1. Real Game

You are your first and most valuable investment. Before you chase status, money, or validation, take care of your body, your mind, and your peace. There's no check big enough to cash out your potential early.

2. Financial Focus

Avoiding costly mistakes is part of building wealth. Every poor choice has a price — from incarceration, to addiction, to teen parenthood. Your health, your freedom, and your focus are all assets. Protect them like you would your bank account.

3. Action Step

Write down three things you've done recently that invested in your future. Then write down one habit, one person, or one distraction that could cost you everything. Make a decision this week to subtract what drains you and double down on what grows you.

4. Quote to Carry

"You are the asset."

You're the brand, the blueprint, the business, and the legacy. Act like it. Move like it. Protect it.

Chapter 11: Your Story Ain't Over

Some stories take a little more time to find their meaning. Some chapters don't make complete sense until years later. But hear me when I tell you this:

Your story ain't over.

I know exactly what it's like to feel stuck. To feel like you've messed up one too many times, hurt too many people, or gone a little bit too far. I've been in that place where every mistake echoes louder than your potential. Where silence becomes your only companion. Where you wonder if the version of you that still dares to dream is even worth believing in anymore.

If you've ever been there, then this chapter is dedicated to you.

To those who are locked away far from home.

On probation.

Out on bond.

Kicked out.

Written off.

Told you were “just like your daddy” or “never gonna amount to anything.”

This is for the ones still breathing, but barely alive.

The Letter That Changed Me

I didn’t expect to be hearing from Poe again. Not after all these years, all the moves, all the silence.

But one day a letter showed up to my house, thick and creased, postmarked from the state pen. It was from Poe. His handwriting was still smooth. It was like his words had rhythm, even from behind bars.

> “Lil man,

The game taught me how to survive, but it never taught me how to stop running. How to really make a place for myself in this world.

Now I’m sitting here, behind these walls, with all this time to think, and I can't help but to keep wondering what could've been different if I would've slowed down sooner. If I would've just got out.

I still got lessons in me though. But you, Meer,

You still got time.

Don’t waste it chasing ghosts like I did.

Use it to build something real. Use it to make something of yourself.

Stay up, kid.

—Poe”

Man, I read that letter about a hundred times.

Not just because I missed him, but because it made something click in my mind.

Time isn't just something that passes from day to day. If you're not building something with it, you're wasting it.

And there's no refund on poorly spent time.

Poe couldn't undo his past. But he was trying to hand me a blueprint for my future.

Jay's Second Shot

That same week, my little cousin Jay hit me up too.

He was only fifteen.

Already on probation.

Already been through two group homes.

He was one more fight away from being locked up again.

I remember when he used to look up to me.

Now I was trying to be someone worthy of being looked up to.

He sent me a picture of himself.

They let him wear a grey jumpsuit—a juvie jumpsuit.

But in the picture, he had something else in his hand.

A notebook.

He had drawn a hoodie with the words “Second Shot” across the front.

Underneath it, he wrote:

> “They got us making career plans in here.

I told them I wanna start my own clothing brand when I get out.

I’ma call it ‘Second Shot.’

You told me not to let this moment define me.

And I didn’t.

I’m still gon’ be something.

Still gon' make a difference."

I stared at that message like it was a Bible scripture.

It hit me hard. Because this was a blueprint too.

Not just for me.

But for anybody out there trying to rewrite their next chapter.

I stared at that text like it was a Bible scripture.

Because my little cousin Jay wasn't supposed to believe in anything anymore.

But here he was, believing in that hoodie idea. In his own brand.

In that second shot.

That's what you call legacy work. Right there in that concrete classroom, surrounded by locked doors, calendars, and slow clocks.

Real Life Reinvention: The Blueprint in Action

This ain't just motivational talk. People are really doing it. Let me give you some real examples.

Coss Marte — This guy used to run one of the biggest drug operations in New York. By the time he got locked up, he was making over 2 million dollars a year. But behind that money was paranoia, betrayal, and a countdown to getting caught. And he did end up getting busted.

But while he was in prison, Coss started working out in his cell. Bodyweight exercises. No equipment. Just discipline and self-determination. He got in shape, then had an idea: What if I turn this into a fitness program when I get out?

Now, he owns ConBody, a prison-style bootcamp gym in New York City that's made over a million dollars in revenue. And he hires other formerly incarcerated people to train the clients too. He flipped his sentence into a six-figure opportunity.

Dr. Stanley Andrisse — He was caught up in the streets, sentenced to ten years for drug trafficking. But while he was locked up, something sparked inside him. He started studying biology, reading textbooks, writing letters to different universities.

When he got out, he went back to school. Finished undergrad, got a PhD in endocrinology. Today, he's a professor at Howard University College of Medicine, researching diabetes and mentoring students.

He went from a prison ID number to Doctor.

He said, "My past does not define me. But it taught me how to focus."

Meek Mill — He was locked up on a probation violation. Could've let it break him. But instead, he became a national voice for criminal justice reform. His net worth is around 20 million dollars. He's not just rapping. He's funding change.

These are just three names. There are more. Plenty more. But I give you these three so you can understand that reinvention is real. Financial comeback is possible.

You Are Not Too Far Gone

Let me say this plainly.

You are not broken.

You are not a mistake.

You are not your charges, your past, or your worst day.

You are merely a work in progress.

And the beauty of progress is that it doesn’t have to be perfect. It just has to keep moving.

So if you’re reading this, still breathing, and still questioning what’s next, that's good. That means you’re still in the fight.

You can start where you are.

Even from a jail cell.

Even from a cot in a homeless shelter.

Even from your grandma's couch or a school suspension.

Your story ain't over.

And you're still holding the pen.

Just start back writing.

Comeback Moves

Let me give you some real tools. Moves you can make even from the bottom:

1. Creative Writing

Start journaling your experiences. Rap. Poetry. Spoken word. Write letters.

Your pain can produce power.

The pages won't judge you. In fact, they'll set you free.

2. Set Goals

Not dreams. Goals.

Real ones. With dates. And action steps.

"I want to launch a clothing brand by 17. This is how I plan to do it."

"I want to pay off this fine in six months. These are ways I can make it happen."

3. Practice Self-Discipline

Start small.

Make your bed in the morning.

Work out in your room for an hour a day.

Read at least 10 pages every day.

Respect structure. It's a great building tool.

4. Study Business Moves

Learn what LLC means. Understand how a brand is built.

Start thinking like the boss you're about to become, not the worker they've always expected you to be.

5. Reflect With Purpose

Every night, ask yourself:

“What did I learn today?”

“What do I want to do better tomorrow?”

6. Learn About Leverage

You don’t always need money. You need strategy.

You could use social media to promote your ideas.

Learn drop-shipping or digital resale.

Look up youth entrepreneur grants.

You can turn nothing into something. The game is out there.

Redemption. Reinvention. Legacy.

Redemption means taking something damaged and making it valuable again.

Your past doesn't disqualify you. It's your power source. The place from which you draw your inspiration.

People don’t need your perfection. They need your process. They need you to keep going.

Reinvention means letting go of who you were so you can become who you’re meant to be.

That means shedding identities that no longer fit.

You’re not a failure. You’re still growing into the person you were put on this earth to be.

Change your habits. Change your circles. Change your outcome.

Legacy means planting seeds that outlive you.

Jay's "Second Shot" wasn't just a design. It was a declaration of his intentions.

He was telling the world he's not done. That he will be remembered. That his life will matter.

You've got that in you too.

Even if nobody ever told you that you do.

Your Next Sentence

Let's end this chapter with a reminder.

You don't get to rewrite your past. But you do get to author your next scene.

And the pen, like I said earlier, it's still in your hand.

You can start your brand.

You can change your surroundings.

You can study the laws that once trapped you and turn them into a business that provides you a path forward.

You can be the one who breaks the cycle.

So don’t let anybody tell you that it’s too late.

Not your P.O.

Not your ex.

Not even the old you.

Your story ain’t over.

It’s just starting to get good.

Let’s write the rest together.

Let’s make it one they’ll never forget.

Keys to the Chapter: Your Story Ain’t Over

1. Real Game:

Your past doesn't cancel your potential. Mistakes don't make you unworthy, they make you human. The difference between staying stuck and writing a comeback is one decision:the decision to keep going.

2. Financial Focus – Redemption Has a ROI:

Even from the bottom, you can build. Your value doesn't disappear with a bad charge or a setback. Learn some skills. Study brands. Build something meaningful. Your future net worth will be a reflection of your internal self-worth.

3. Action Step:

Pick one thing you've been through that you're ashamed of, now , write a paragraph about how you survived it. Then ask yourself: how could this experience help somebody else? Your story is your currency. Don't waste it.

4. Quote to Carry:

"You don't get to rewrite your past. But you do get to author your next scene."

Chapter 12: The Real Flex Is Freedom

Growing up, I always thought the ultimate goal was to get money and be seen.

Nice shoes. Some flashy jewelry. A million social media followers. Having everybody know who you are before you ever even walk in the room. That's what I thought winning looked like. That's what we were all chasing.

But what if I told you that that's not it? That's not actually the goal at all.

Because I've seen people with all those things—the drip, the followers, the cars, the clout—still losing at life. Still broke (mentally, spiritually, and emotionally). Still trapped. Still empty.

That's when I thought to myself, the flex isn't being watched. It's being at peace.

Let me break that down for you, like I wish somebody had done for me: freedom is the real definition of wealth.

Not just physical freedom, like freedom from a cell, but mental freedom. Freedom from the pressure to perform. Emotional freedom from toxic cycles—people, places, and things. And financial freedom from debt and desperation.

Let's talk about that.

What "Flexin" Really Means

Too many people spend their lives trying to impress the same people who wouldn't help them if they fell right in front of them.

They spend money they don't have, to buy things they don't need, to prove something that doesn't really matter.

Looking rich has become more important than really being rich, or really being free.

But the real ones—the smart ones—they move differently. They build quietly. They understand that peace is power.

Because here's the truth about it:

Loud money doesn't last.

Real wealth doesn't need a spotlight. It never did.

And flexing isn't about what's in your hand. It's about the quality of your life.

So, do you really wanna know what flexing looks like?

It looks like waking up when you want to.

Taking care of your mama and your family without going broke in the process.

Saying "no" to what doesn't align with your morals and values.

Owning your time, your name, and your decisions.

Now that's the real flex.

Physical Freedom, Don't Lose That

There's nothing scarier than being physically trapped. Jail. Juvie. Prison. Believe me, you don't wanna experience that.

You might think that one charge won't hurt you. That sliding with your homies just once ain't gonna change your life.

But here's the truth about it—it only takes one night to lose everything. I've seen people wind up serving a life sentence because they didn't have the courage to tell their buddies, "No, I can't ride with you on this one."

You don't want to be the kid writing home from a prison cell, wondering what your life could've been like if you had just walked away.

And I'm not preaching from a high horse. I'm talking from the trenches. I've been on the other side of that line. Seen the inside of those walls. Watched friends lose decades to mistakes that took seconds.

You're not soft for protecting your freedom. You're smart.

Freedom from Obligations That Own You

Let's be 100 about it.

Sometimes the thing that traps you isn't the law—it's the people you're running with.

The very gangs that claim to love you but ask you to risk your life every day just to prove you belong. Partners that call you "real" only when you're ready to sacrifice your entire future for them. Friends that keep you stuck in cycles of destruction simply because they're scared to grow.

And let's be honest about something else too. Having a child before you're ready can potentially alter the direction of the remainder of your life.

Ain't nothing wrong with love. But being tied down before you truly ever even get to know who you are—that's a cost too many of us are forced to pay without really understanding the price.

You don't owe anybody else your future. You don't owe the block your potential. You don't have to sell your peace of mind to afford the cost of popularity.

The realest love you'll ever show your people is being around for them—whole, healthy, focused, and free.

If that's not enough? Then you need to be asking yourself if they're really your people to begin with.

Freedom from Addiction and Distraction

Let's talk about it.

Drugs, alcohol, pornography, pills, fast food, gambling, even social media—anything that keeps you numb instead of focused can be labeled a trap.

You might think it's just "chilling out" or "blowing off a little steam." But over time, that fog creeps into other areas of your day-to-day life.

Then, before you realize it, your energy is gone. Your clarity is gone. Your grind is gone.

You can't build your empire if your mind is always cloudy. It takes clarity and focus to be the kind of boss we're training ourselves to be, Youngster.

Besides, you deserve a clear head. A strong body. A focused spirit. Don't give that up for a moment of escape.

Temporary escape feels good, but true freedom is good permanently.

Time and Money: The Freedom You Can Build

Let me ask you something:

If you had enough money to never clock into another job again, what would you do with your life?

Would you travel? Would you buy your mom a house? Would you teach your little cousin how to code? What would you do?

That's the kind of freedom I'm talking about. The kind you build—not the kind you beg for.

Passive income. Ownership. Leverage.

Freedom is knowing your bills are covered even when you're sleeping.

Not because someone gave you a handout, but because you studied the game, made the necessary moves, and created something bigger than yourself.

That's what people like Nipsey Hussle understood.

Nipsey Hussle: A Blueprint for Freedom

Nip wasn't just a rapper. He was a strategist. A businessman. A community builder. A truly revolutionary thinker.

He bought up the block he once hustled on. Turned a strip mall into a hub for his operations. Opened The Marathon Clothing store right where he used to struggle. Employed people from his community that needed second chances. And he thrived.

He didn't just rap about change—he invested in it.

He preached real ownership, not just success. He made sure the people around him were learning how to eat for life—not just when he fed them. He didn't flex with chains. He flexed with equity.

And when you asked him what he wanted, it wasn't clout. It was freedom.

(I pray God grants him paradise.)

LeBron James: Freedom to Empower Others

LeBron is a whole billionaire now. (Probably a couple times over by the time you read this.) But his biggest move was opening a school.

The "I PROMISE" school in Akron, Ohio gives kids from tough backgrounds a chance to be something more. He didn't stop with shoes and endorsements. He put real money into real change.

LeBron understands that freedom means giving back to those who can benefit from the help you're in the position to offer.

He could've just played ball and stacked money. Instead, he invested in education, housing, family support systems, and mental health resources for his people.

Because what good is your success if the people who look like you—or look up to you—stay stuck?

That's the kind of wealth we're doing all this for. That's the kind of flex that lasts generations.

Money Ain't the End Goal, Freedom Is

Let's be clear.

Money is not the goal. It's a tool to help you reach the goal.

The goal is:

Peace

Purpose

Self-respect

Sustainability

The ability to say yes to what fuels you and no to what drains you.

When your worth isn't tied to your bank account or your likes, you move differently.

You work smarter. You live better. You treat people with more love, dignity, and respect.

Because then you're not hustling for approval—you're building for a lasting impact.

So What Does Freedom Look Like?

It looks like having dinner with your family without stressing about where the next meal will be coming from.

It looks like turning your phone off for a weekend and not worrying about missing money.

It looks like waking up with ideas, not anxiety.

It looks like walking away from bad deals and bad energy and not starving because of it.

It looks like clarity—mentally, spiritually, and emotionally.

Steps Toward Freedom

Here's how you start:

1. Learn to Budget. Know where your money is going. Track it. Learn it. Control it.

2. Build Something. Start a side hustle, drop a design, teach a skill, make some content. Whatever it is, just be sure you own it.

3. Eliminate Dead Weight. Get away from unproductive people. Break bad habits. Don't spend wastefully. Clean up the way you think. No negativity. Avoid anything that slows you down.

4. Get Mentors, Dead or Alive. Study great minds. Learn from people like Nipsey, LeBron, Dr. Claude Anderson—even local legends. You don't have to know them to grow from them.

5. Dream Bigger Than Just Money. Write your personal definition of freedom. Be specific. Then chase that, not just a dollar sign.

Legacy Is the Endgame

Because this freedom isn't just for you.

It's for your little brother watching how you move. For your future kids. For the young homies on the corner that look up to you.

When you're moving with purpose, they're learning to do the same.

There's always somebody watching how you move.

That's what Nip meant by "The Marathon." It's not about speed. It's about endurance. It's about passing the baton to the generations after us.

You're building so they don't have to start from scratch.

You're healing so they don't inherit all the pain you've had to endure.

You're investing so they don’t just survive, they can thrive.

That’s real freedom. That’s generational flexin.

Final Word: Choose Peace Over Popularity

The world is probably gonna tell you to chase the attention.

But I’m telling you to chase alignment.

Choose peace over pressure. Put discipline over distractions. Value freedom over flexin.

Because you’re not just building a life, you’re building a legacy.

And the goal is to live in a way that feels good, not just looks good.

Hold on to your freedom like it’s sacred. Because it is.

And one day, when the chains come off, not just from your wrists, but from your mind, you’ll realize,

The realest flex… is being free.

Keys to the Chapter: The Real Flex is Freedom

1. Real Game

The biggest flex isn't designer belts or social media clout. It's peace. It's being able to walk away from chaos, to say no to what drains you, and live a life that doesn't need a filter to feel good.

2. Financial Focus , Peace Over Pressure

Wealth isn't loud. It's quiet. It's in the ability to turn your phone off without fear. It's freedom from check-to-check living. It's owning your time, building assets, and walking away from any deal that doesn't align with your peace and purpose.

3. Action Step

Write out your personal definition of freedom. Not the version they sold you. Your version. Be real with it. Then write down one thing you can start doing this week to move closer to it.

4. Quote to Carry

"Loud money doesn't last. Real wealth doesn't need a spotlight.

The realest flex is being free."

Chapter 13: The Blueprint

If you're reading this right now, you've made it further than most people already.

And not just in this book, but in life in general. Because most people don't finish things. They start hungry but then give up and fall off when it gets a little uncomfortable. You though, you stayed the course. That alone tells me that you're built differently.

You're not here by accident. You were meant to make it to this point.

And now that you've soaked up some high level game, some fundamental life lessons, some all-around realness — what are you gonna do with it?

Because this book wasn't just about money. It was about understanding the world in which we live. It was about recognizing your self-worth. It was about finding freedom. It was about getting to know the real you.

And now, it's time to build.

You Are the Architect of Your Life

Everything starts with you. Your mindset. Your habits. Your energy.

Nobody's coming to save you, Youngster. But you don't need to be saved. You just need to remember who you are.

You are the brand. You are the business. You are the bank. You are the investment.

So act like you are. Walk like you are. Think like you are. Move like you are.

That means you don't just wake up hoping things change for you out of the blue. You wake up and change them, on purpose.

You draw up your plan. You control the way you spend your time. You speak with purpose. You walk towards your legacy.

And when the world tries to tell you that you're not enough, you remind it:

"I'm not only enough, I'm more than enough."

Legacy Over Likes

Stop building for applause. Start building for a lasting impact.

Nobody remembers who had the most followers. But they remember who made the deepest mark.

You don't need everyone to clap. You just need to keep planting seeds.

And always remember:

Your name matters.

Your vision matters.

Your family's future depends on your discipline.

Because one smart move today can feed your entire bloodline tomorrow.

Ownership is how you win.

Equity is how you last.

We're not chasing temporary fame. We're chasing forever freedom.

And real freedom starts in the mind.

The Blueprint: 10 Codes to Build By

1. You are the asset. Invest in yourself first, always. It all starts and ends with you. If you're not in the game, then none of this other stuff matters. Look out for your star player.

2. Build before you flex. Flexing feels good now. Freedom is good forever. There will be time to shine on the world later. First, we need to establish ourselves.

3. Create more than you consume. The world needs your gifts, not just your appetite. Don't run through the bag as soon as it touches your hands. Don't take away more than you're giving. The game will remember you for what you gave, not what you kept.

4. Protect your peace. Not everyone deserves access to your energy. Some people shouldn’t even be allowed in your space. They don’t add value, but they will rob you of your peace. Don’t allow that.

5. Keep your credit clean. It’s your name on paper. Guard it. Ain't nothing like keeping your word solid. When you say something, stand on it. When you borrow, repay what you owe. A good name is worth more than money.

6. Own your time. Don’t just clock in. Time is money. Ownership allows you to spend more of it on the things that matter most to you.

7. Heal before you lead. Don't pass your pain down. Pass the game down. Move with the right intentions. Don't lead others into a war they don't understand.

8. Surround yourself with visionaries. Friends should multiply your mission, not subtract from it. Keep smart, qualified, and loyal people in your corner. They're a valuable commodity.

9. Pray often. It's free. It's powerful. It works. Nothing else needs to be said on this.

10. Remember who you are. Royalty. Legacy. Vision. You're the one your ancestors prayed for. Do what you're supposed to be doing.

Top-Level Game: Simplified

Compound interest: Money that makes money over time. Start early—even five dollars a week adds up.

Leverage: Using one thing (money, relationships, knowledge) to multiply your reach.

Assets vs. Liabilities: Buy what brings money in, not just what takes it out.

Ownership: If you don't own it, you can't pass it down. Period.

Faith: The original superpower. With it, you'll move mountains nobody thought possible.

Real Talk: You Weren't Even Supposed to Learn This

There was a time in our history when it was illegal to teach Black people how to read. They knew it would make it impossible to keep you a slave if you learned too much. Knowledge is the key, Youngster.

Let that sink in.

Just the act of gaining knowledge was dangerous. Hell, it was illegal for you. That's how powerful your mind is. That's how scared these systems have always been of your understanding.

Why? Because a Black child who learns to read... becomes a teen who starts to think... becomes a man or woman who starts to lead.

And on an even playing field, you're tough to contend with.

And nothing is more dangerous to a broken system than a free-thinking, well-read, deeply grounded person of color.

You've just joined a lineage of warriors, thinkers, kings, queens, revolutionaries, and builders.

Use what you know to uplift those who follow you.

Choose Your Circle Carefully

Your crew can be a blessing or a bullet. You have to be careful to watch the energy around you.

If your friends mock your dreams, let them go. The same way faith can open any door, doubt can close it. Only roll with those who have supreme confidence in you. They'll do what's necessary to help you achieve your goals.

If your circle doesn't talk about growth, faith, legacy, freedom—switch it up. Negative circles are a tremendous waste of your valuable time. Birds of a feather flock together. Fly with the eagles. Don't pluck amongst turkeys.

You become like the people you're around. So be around people building. Be around people with purpose. Be around people who want to win with you—not against you.

Be mindful of the ones who are secretly in competition with you. They're potential enemies.

Iron sharpens iron. But rust infects.

Choose wisely.

Prayer Is Free. So Is Vision

Don't let anybody tell you being spiritual is soft.

Pray like your future depends on it—because it does.

There’s power in the Divine. There’s clarity in faith. There’s direction in silence.

You’re not just a physical being. You’re spiritual. Mental. Eternal.

When you don’t know what move to make, pray. Ask for clarity and direction. When you feel alone—pray. When the dream feels too big—pray. And when you're winning—pray.

Stay prayed up. It's a powerful tool and it'll give you peace.

Because if you’re connected to something higher, there’s no limit to how high you can rise.

Final Words: This Is Just the Beginning

Your story doesn’t end here. This was never just a book. It’s been a mirror this whole time. It’s a map. It’s a mission.

You’ve got what you need:

The mindset

The language

The principles

The fire

Now it’s time to move forward into your purpose.

It’s time to build. It’s time to rise.

And if nobody else tells you this today—I see you. I believe in you. I wrote this for you.

And above all else,

I love you.

I didn’t write this just to inspire you to dream, but to show you what you could do.

You don’t have to follow the same cycle as everyone else. You can start a new legacy. You can be the reason your family sees the other side of the struggle.

And remember this:

You were born more than enough. You are the blueprint.

Now go build something monumental.

Keys to the Chapter: The Blueprint

1. Real Game:

You are not just a product of your environment. You are the architect of your life. You can build a future that's bigger than your past. Not because it's easy, but because you finally see yourself as worth the effort.

2. Financial Focus Legacy Over Likes:

A strong brand outlives a viral moment. Stop building for applause. Start building for ownership, freedom, and generational impact. Money is cool, but legacy is lasting power. That's the wealth that never depreciates.

3. Action Step:

Write down a blueprint for your next 90 days. Be specific. What habits do you need to create? What distractions do you need to eliminate? What one thing can you start building right now that'll benefit your future self?

4. Quote to Carry

"You are the brand. You are the business. You are the bank. You are the investment."

Say that until it sinks in. Then move like it's true—because it is!

GLOSSARY OF TERMS

Asset:

Something that puts money in your pocket—either now or in the future.

Bitcoin:

The first and most well-known cryptocurrency. A digital form of money not controlled by any government or bank.

Blockchain:

A secure, digital ledger where transactions are recorded publicly and permanently.

Bonds:

A loan you give to a company or government that they pay back with interest.

Brand:

Your name, image, product, or vibe that people recognize and trust.

Budget:

A plan for how your money moves.

Business Entity:

A legally recognized structure for your hustle.

Compound Interest:

Interest that earns on top of itself. Money that makes money over time.

Credit:

Your financial reputation. A score showing how well you handle borrowed money.

Credit Utilization:

The percentage of your credit limit you use. Keep it under 30% for better scores.

Cryptocurrency:

A digital currency that uses cryptography to secure transactions. Examples include Bitcoin, Ethereum, and Solana.

Debt:

Money you owe that drains your income. Can be used strategically or destructively.

Decentralization

Power or control spread out. In crypto, no single person or bank runs the show.

Digital Asset:

Anything online that has value and can be owned or sold.

Digital Real Estate:

Online spaces you control, like a website, domain, or NFT gallery.

Dividends:

Payouts to investors from company profits.

Drop-shipping:

Selling items online without holding any inventory.

EIN (Employer Identification Number):

A tax ID for your business. It's your business's Social Security number.

Entrepreneur:

Someone who builds a business, not just a job.

Equity:

Ownership in something valuable, real estate, a brand, a company.

Ethereum:

A major blockchain used for smart contracts, NFTs, and decentralized apps.

Fiat Currency:

Money made by governments. Example: U.S. dollars, euros.

Financial Freedom

When your money makes more money than your job does.

Fractional Shares:

Small portions of a stock so you can invest with limited funds.

Gas Fee:

The small cost to complete a transaction on a blockchain like Ethereum.

Generational Possibilities:

The future you unlock for your people by planting seeds today.

Generational Wealth:

Assets, income, and wisdom passed down.

Grants:

Free money for school, business, or projects that align with certain missions.

High-Yield Savings Account:

A savings account that grows faster by earning higher interest.

Income vs. Wealth:

Income is what you make. Wealth is what you keep, invest, and pass on.

Insurance Policy (Whole Life):

Pays your family when you die and builds cash value while you live.

Intellectual Property (IP):

Your original work, music, writing, logos, designs, that has legal and money value.

Investment:

Putting time, money, or energy into something that should grow.

Leverage:

Using a small resource (credit, connections) to make a big move.

Liability:

Anything that takes money out of your pocket. The opposite of an asset.

Licensing:

Letting someone pay to use your work while you keep ownership.

LLC (Limited Liability Company):

A legal business structure that protects your personal money.

Marketing:

Telling the world what you do and why they should care.

Net Worth:

Assets minus liabilities. The real scoreboard of wealth.

NFT (Non-Fungible Token):

A unique, ownable digital file. Like art, music, or writing—stored on the blockchain.

Ownership:

Legal control of something valuable. If you own it, you eat from it.

Passive Income:

Money that shows up while you sleep—royalties, rent, investments.

Private Key:

A secret code that unlocks your crypto wallet. Lose it, lose everything.

Profit:

The money you keep after all costs are paid.

Profit Margin:

The percent of revenue that turns into profit.

Public Key:

Your safe-to-share crypto wallet address.

Return on Investment (ROI):

How much you gain from what you put in.

Revenue:

All money brought in before costs are taken out.

Savings:

Money stored—not spent—for future moves or emergencies.

Self-Worth:

Knowing what you bring to the table. It shapes how you charge, speak, and lead.

Side Hustle

Extra streams of income. A seed that can grow into your main thing.

Smart Contract:

Code that runs itself when conditions are met. Example: NFT sales that auto-send royalties.

Smart Wallet:

A crypto wallet that holds your assets and connects you to Web3 platforms.

Solana:

A fast, low-fee blockchain used for NFTs, tokens, and apps.

Stablecoin:

Crypto tied to stable value (like $1). Used for safe moves in a volatile space.

Sustainability:

Doing it big—but in a way that lasts. No burnout. No backtracking.

Tax:

The government's share of your money. Understand it to legally protect your bag.

Tax Bracket:

The percent you pay in taxes based on how much you make.

Token:

A digital unit of value. It can represent ownership, access, or rights.

Web3:

The internet where users own their own data, wallets, and brands.

Whitepaper:

The official breakdown of a crypto project. Read it before you invest.

CHAPTER TEMPLATES (In Book Flow)

TO PROMOTE ENGAGEMENT

1. Risk/Reward Assessment Table

Placement: After Chapter 1 – Poe Dad

Purpose: Helps readers think critically about the cost of choices

Fields:

Move

Best Outcome

Worst Outcome

Is the risk worth it?

2. Dream-to-Plan Worksheet

Placement: After Chapter 2 – More Than One Way Out

Purpose: Helps readers define and map out their vision

Fields:

My dream

Why it matters

What I already have

What I need

First 3 steps

Deadline

3. Money Habits Tracker

Placement: After Chapter 6 – Money Ain't the Answer, But It Opens Doors

Purpose: Develops awareness around spending and saving

Fields:

Date

Money In

Money Out

What I spent it on

Need or Want

What I learned

4. Skill-to-Hustle Builder

Placement: After Chapter 7 – Own or Be Owned

Purpose: Helps readers monetize skills and talents

Fields:

Skill

Problem it solves

Who needs it

First step

What to charge

5. Minpdset Shift Journal

Placement: After Chapter 8 – Rich Starts in the Mind

Purpose: Replaces limiting thoughts with empowering beliefs

Fields:

Old thought

Why it held me back

New thought

Action I'll take

6. Asset vs. Liability Chart

Placement: After Chapter 10 – You Are the Asset

Purpose: Clarifies what's helping vs hurting their financial growth

Fields:

Assets

Liabilities

7. Freedom Formula Prompts

Placement: After Chapter 12 – Real Freedom

Purpose: Defines peace, purpose, and freedom in practical terms

Fields:

What brings me peace

How much time I control

What I want to own

What I must let go

8. Legacy Builder Framework

Placement: After Chapter 13 – Poe Dad No Dad

Purpose: Focuses the reader on generational wealth and vision

Fields:

What I want to leave behind

Who it benefits

What tools I need

How I’ll protect it

Be referenced at the end of each chapter.

About the Author

Almeer Nance is a powerful voice for transformation, financial empowerment, and generational healing. Born and raised in the Lonsdale neighborhood of Knoxville, Tennessee, Almeer faced challenges early in life that many never overcome. Sentenced to life plus 25 years as a juvenile, he refused to let the system define his future.

Instead, he used his time to study, grow, and lead. Through self-education and the support of transformative prison education programs like THEI and CEI, Almeer earned his associate degree, a technical degree from TCAT, and his bachelor's degree from Lane College—all while incarcerated.

His story and mission have been featured in outlets such as Al Jazeera English and Tennessee Lookout, where he speaks about juvenile justice, hope, and the power of rewriting your life story. He is a mentor, educator, and voice for youth who've been overlooked or written off.

With Poe Dad No Dad, Almeer doesn't just tell his story—he shares strategy, wisdom, and real-life principles. Financial literacy, spiritual growth, and practical lessons are woven together with culture, pain, love, and legacy. His message is clear: no matter where you start, you can still build something legendary.

Almeer is fighting daily to combat the idea that the lives of our children are of no consequence. He stands as living proof that even those who've made horrible mistakes have the capability and capacity to grow and change—if given the tools, and the opportunity.

He is a blueprint that greatness can grow in the most unlikely places

Summary

Poe Dad No Dad is more than a memoir, it's a manual, a manifesto, a mirror.

Written by Almeer Kilee, a man forged by the fire of poverty, abandonment, and incarceration, this book speaks directly to the ones the system forgot — the youth raised by the streets, the dreamers drowning in debt, and the kids who never saw themselves in the pages of the books handed to them in school.

Told with raw honesty and unfiltered wisdom, this isn't just a story about a missing father, it's about missing foundations, missing blueprints, and the consequences of being left to figure life out alone. Each chapter blends personal storytelling with real-life financial game, from how to flip pain into passive income, to how to reclaim ownership of your story, your name, and your future.

This book teaches credit, assets, digital currency, mindset, and legacy in a way that feels real, because it is.

For every reader who grew up without trust funds, but with trust issues. For every young mind raised in broken homes, but still hungry to build something whole. This book is for you.

www.ingramcontent.com/pod-product-compliance
Lightning Source LLC
LaVergne TN
LVHW022212200926
848481LV00006B/1944